a meaningful
MESS

April-
Thank you so
much for
the work
you do!
Be BRAVE!

♥ Dede
McNai

PS Had fun learning
w/ you in
Jacksonville. :)

A Teacher's Guide to Student-Driven Classrooms, Authentic Learning, Student Empowerment, and Keeping It All Together…*Without Losing Your Mind*

a meaningful
MESS

Andi McNair

PRUFROCK PRESS INC.
WACO, TEXAS

Library of Congress Cataloging-in-Publication Data

Names: McNair, Andi, 1977- author.
Title: A meaningful mess : a teacher's guide to student-driven classrooms,
   authentic learning, student empowerment, and keeping it all together
   without losing your mind / Andi McNair.
Description: Waco, TX : Prufrock Press Inc., [2019] | Includes
   bibliographical references.
Identifiers: LCCN 2019003412 (print) | LCCN 2019016885 (ebook) | ISBN
   9781618218421 (eBook) | ISBN 9781618218414 (pbk.)
Subjects: LCSH: Student-centered learning--Study and teaching. | Blended
   learning. | Generation Z. | Classroom management.
Classification: LCC LB1027.23 (ebook) | LCC LB1027.23 .M396 2019 (print) |
   DDC 371.39--dc23
LC record available at https://lccn.loc.gov/2019003412

Edited by Katy McDowall

Cover and layout design by Allegra Denbo
Cover illustration by Micah Benson

ISBN-13: 978-1-61821-841-4

Printed in the United States of America.

At the time of this book's publication, all facts and figures cited are the most current available. All telephone numbers, addresses, and website URLs are accurate and active. All publications, organizations, websites, and other resources exist as described in the book, and all have been verified. The authors and Prufrock Press Inc. make no warranty or guarantee concerning the information and materials given out by organizations or content found at websites, and we are not responsible for any changes that occur after this book's publication. If you find an error, please contact Prufrock Press Inc.

Prufrock Press Inc.
P.O. Box 8813
Waco, TX 76714-8813
Phone: (800) 998-2208
Fax: (800) 240-0333
http://www.prufrock.com

Table of Contents

Acknowledgments

I am so thankful to so many people who have helped me learn and grow as a person and an educator. I believe so many of the things that I believe because of people who have taken the time to invest in me. This book is a result of those investments. I could never put into words how thankful I am for my sweet family, friends, and colleagues who have held my hand on this journey.

My husband, John—Thank you so much for always listening to my crazy ideas and supporting me in every single dream that I pursue. I love you more than you'll ever know!

My children, Cory, Eli, and Katy—You are the reason that I do what I do. I can't wait to see what your futures hold and how you use what you've learned to be amazing!

My parents, Ann and Ronnie Richardson—Your love and support means everything, and I could never do what I do without everything that you've taught me along the way.

My sister, Mandi Killough—Thank you for listening and being my best friend. I am so thankful for our conversations and the relationship that we have as adults.

Kari Espin and Jaime Donally—You girls have no idea the impact that you have had on me and my career. Just knowing you is an inspiration and I am so thankful for our friendships. I love our conversations about change and the passion that we all share for creating real change that will impact classrooms all over the world!

My PLN—I learn from you all every single day, and the connections that I've made on social media have changed so much for me. I think of all of you as friends, and I'm grateful for your passion and willingness to share what you do and why you do it.

Katy McDowall—Thank you again for your patience and guidance. Your flexibility and attention to detail makes this process so much easier!

My Region 12 Family—I am so thankful to work for an organization that supports me in all of my endeavors and is passionate about doing what it takes to provide real, relevant professional development for educators. Your support drives so much of what I do, and I appreciate every single one of you!

I am also so thankful for God's grace and blessings, as it is only through Him that my mess is made meaningful.

What Makes a Mess Meaningful?

"THIS is a mess!" Those were my exact words after I decided to allow my classroom to be not only student-centered, but also student-driven. I made the decision to allow my students to learn by doing and to give them opportunities to learn by pursuing their own passions. In doing so, everything looked differently than it had before. Managing the classroom was no longer easy, predictable, and comfortable. Instead, it was difficult, risky, and uncomfortable. I wondered if I had made the wrong decision and considered going back to expecting my students to sit quietly, listen while I taught, and then regurgitate on a worksheet or a unit test the information that I had shared in order to prove that they had "learned" the content.

The reality is that I was way out of my lane and felt like I could lose control at any moment. The new strategies I was employing in the classroom were unfamiliar and not as easy as what I had done before. To put it simply, I was outside of my comfort zone, and because of that, I felt vulnerable and questioned my decision. But the truth is, none of us should be comfortable in education right now. If educating today's students is comfortable and easy, something is wrong. Considering the skills and strengths of today's learners and the access that they have to the world, we should be doing things in the classroom that are different and beyond what we have always known.

That's the purpose of this book—to provide you with strategies to empower today's learners. How? To get started, you must be ready to take risks in the classroom, practice messy learning, seek meaningful work, and find meaning (and fun) amongst a mess.

Take Risks in the Classroom

Allowing students to learn by doing while pursuing their passions requires risk-taking. Taking a risk can be very scary, but the reality is that if we never take the risk, we will never see the reward. Comfort zones can be a scary place where nothing ever happens. They are very easy to fall into and very hard to get out of. It is only when we begin to push past our comfort zones and take risks that we will begin to give this generation of learners what they need to experience real learning. Continuing to teach the way that we have in the past simply will not work for today's students. And why would it? We are preparing today's learners for a completely different society and completely different real-world experiences than students from even a decade ago.

You don't have to look far to realize that things are changing. When we eat out at restaurants, we no longer have to wait for a waiter to bring us our ticket. Instead, we are able to pay immediately using the mini-kiosk on our table. Self-driving cars are no longer things that are just talked about; they exist. We can interact with images and text using augmented reality, bringing images to life. There's no denying that things have changed, and because society has changed, so have our learners. Never before have learners had instant access to information and the opportunity to instantly share their learning with others around the world. That, in and of itself, is reason for change. For so long, our role as educators has been to deliver information. Because students now have instant access to that information, it only makes sense that what we do as educators must be reconsidered.

Today's students need more, and I would even say that they deserve more. The reality is that there are not too many successful companies that have not been willing to take risks. In fact, many of them are successful because of their willingness to take a risk. Blake Mycoskie, the founder of TOMS, took a big risk when he made the decision to build his company around the idea of giving away a pair of shoes for every pair that was purchased (Rampton, 2016). There are many shoe companies, but not many of them make such big promises. Mycoskie knew his customers and knew what he wanted for his company well enough to be willing to do something different. In doing so, he was able to build a reputation, and following that resulted in a successful business that has done and continues to do very well.

> We should expect nothing less than greatness from our learners and do what it takes to set them on their individual paths toward success.

Just like Mycoskie, Elon Musk, Steve Jobs, and Bill Gates became successful because they were willing to think outside of the box and invest in what they believed in. They were unwilling to settle for mediocrity and believed enough in their investments to do whatever it took to make them successful. As educators, we invest in our learners. Just like all of these revolutionary leaders, we should be unwilling to settle for mediocrity. We should expect nothing less than greatness from our learners and do what it takes to set them on their individual paths toward success.

Many of these individuals went through difficulties and confusion while they were figuring things out. However, they knew the reward would be worth the risk—or at least they believed that it would. Although risk-taking can be messy, it is often worth every single struggle, failure, and pitfall that is experienced along the way.

I think many successful investors, inventors, and innovators would say that they were willing . . . willing to step out on a limb, willing to do something different, and willing to try things that are unfamiliar and uncomfortable. In doing so, they found their own passions, helped others, and discovered ways to make the world a better place. You see, willingness is the bridge between doing what has always been done and doing what works. When we are willing, we create a path for change.

Practice Messy Learning, Not Messy Teaching

Let's be real: A mess is not always a good thing. I can think of lots of messes that I try to avoid because there is no purpose or reason for them. For example, it's so frustrating to walk into my kids' rooms and see that they are a complete mess. There's no purpose to that type of mess, and nothing good will come from it. The messier their rooms become, the more work and more time they require. I am by no means a neat freak, but I do know that unproductive messes just cause frustration and anxiety. However, not all messes are meaningless. Some messes are not only meaningful, but also necessary for real change to occur.

In the classroom, things can get messy, but there is a difference between messy learning and messy teaching. When we use the term *messy teaching*, it sends the message that the classroom is messy, the activity is messy, or just the teaching itself is messy. Messy learning is different. Messy learning is the willingness to learn through the experience even when it's difficult or confusing. Learning should be infinite and not always be wrapped in a perfect package with a bow attached. Learning is something that can be delivered, but it often needs to be experienced so that the learner goes after it and does what it takes to reach deeper levels of understanding.

I like to refer to messy learning as a meaningful mess. One of the definitions of a mess is "a situation or state of affairs that is confused or full of difficulties." Confusion and difficulty aren't always negative. Out of confusion can come clarity, and out of difficulty can come a sense of accomplishment or perseverance. Those things do not come when lessons or activities are predictable and easy. It's okay to have a classroom that engages students in messy learning. The key is to make sure that it's a meaningful mess that results in meaningful learning.

> Messy learning is the willingness to learn through the experience even when it's difficult or confusing.

I recently asked several educators about how they would define messy learning. Although they all shared different perspectives, they all alluded to the reality that messy learning is unpredictable and involves the learner having some control and even driving the learning. Figure 1 features their definitions.

Seek Meaningful Work

When teaching is predictable, it becomes mundane. When it becomes mundane, it becomes boring. And when it becomes boring, teachers burn out. None of us want to do things that are not meaningful. Meaningful work is what drives us to get up in the morning and causes us to want to be in the classroom. A passion for what we do is where we find our purpose, and without purpose, it's difficult to justify the why behind what we do.

So what is meaningful work, and how do we find it? Meaningful work is work that is driven by passion. It is work that is inspired by

Messy learning is when you don't know what's going to happen. Instead of you making the plans, the students make the plans. It's sometimes really loud and sometimes really quiet. With messy learning, you never know what's going to happen. And that's okay, as long as it's still learning.

—Joy Kirr

Messy learning is not having boundaries or set rules that students need to follow. The students create those, and sometimes it's what the teacher expects, and more often, it's way better.

—Sarah Gaetano

Messy learning in the classroom involves student choice and allows their voices to be heard. It's a classroom that allows students to flexibly move around and problem solve. Students are able to ask their peers for help, not just the teacher. Messy learning is active learning in which the teacher provides guidelines but lets students decide the process and, in some cases, even the product. It can be loud at times and definitely chaotic, but I think it's organized chaos. All students are engaged, actively participating in their own learning, working at their own level using higher level thinking skills. I can't imagine teaching any other way. To me, messy learning is the way students learn. It's authentic. It's real. It's how classroom learning should be.

—Rebecca Giacopelli

Messy learning is learning by immersion. There is an overall goal, but how the students get there is up to them. It looks different for every student, which means that messy learning meets students where they are. For teachers, messy learning is wanting students to achieve that goal and facilitating to the best of our ability the organized chaos that messy learning can be. It's messy both literally and figuratively. It's frustrating but incredibly cool to see how everything pans out. I think because education is changing, messy learning is something students are good at outside of the classroom. The ultimate goal of messy learning is to empower students.

—Ethan Silva

Messy learning for kids is being so involved and so intense on what you are doing that you're not even paying attention to where you are putting things or where things are falling . . . you are just in the mix. They are just doing something that they are passionate about and then they look around and say, "Oh my goodness, I have a mess to clean up!" And I love that.

—Kimberly Belleisle

Figure 1. Definitions of *messy learning*.

the desire to do what is right rather than what is easy. Meaningful work is empowering and brings confidence and contentment to the person doing the work.

Does this description of meaningful work describe how you feel about teaching? Chances are that it did at one time. However, for whatever reason, you may

> Meaningful work is work that is driven by passion.

have fallen into doing what is predictable and easy instead of what is challenging and messy. You became comfortable with the mundane but realize that being comfortable is very different than being content.

Here are some things to think about:

- Do you wake up in the morning excited about what you have planned for the learners in your classroom?
- If you weren't afraid of failing, what would you try in your classroom?
- What are your strengths and passions as an educator?
- What are you doing as an educator to continue to learn and grow?
- What do you consider "working" in your own classroom?

Some of you might have laughed a little when you read that first question. Excited? You might be thinking, "I wake up in the morning trying to find ways to drag myself out the door to my car so that I can get to my classroom." The word *exciting* is not the word you would use as you think about the activities that you have planned for your students. Let me just say that I know exactly how you feel. I had these exact feelings and thoughts before I changed my mindset and began taking risks to engage my students in a meaningful mess.

Find Meaning (and Fun) Amongst a Mess

Because of what school has become for not only educators, but students as well, it is not often thought of as being fun. Instead, it's seen as something that students must endure in order to become productive members of society. I disagree. I believe that learning can be something that is both meaningful and fun. Throughout this book, I hope to introduce many ways that you can create a classroom that is not only fun and empowering for your students, but also fun and empowering for you as an educator. I will include opportunities to engage, be empowered, and reflect throughout each chapter. I wanted to write a book that was personalized and meaningful to those who were reading it. In order for this to be a personal journey, these calls to action are going to be very important. Let's jump right in.

REFLECT

Think about how you feel in the morning before school. Are you excited? What would it feel like to be excited as you go to school every morning, and how might that impact classroom culture?

_____

_____

_____

_____

There are so many things that we miss out on because we are afraid of failure. We fear that a risky learning experience won't go well or just won't go the way that we expected. This fear of failure keeps so many of us from doing what we know is best for our learners. What if I take this risk and my test scores don't improve? What if I try something new and my students don't like it? What if I do something that I've never done before and the results aren't what I expected? The "what ifs" haunt us and hold us back from doing so many amazing things. But what if you take the risk and scores do improve? What if you try something new and your students love it? What if you do something you have never done before and the results are so much more than you could have imagined?

> Educators who have an intense enthusiasm for what they do each day are the educators who leave the biggest impact on their students.

EMPOWER

What is something that you have wanted to try in your classroom but haven't because of your fear of failure? Take that fear of failure and change your perspective. For example, instead of "What if a Makerspace is just a mess and my students cannot control themselves with that much freedom?" ask yourself, "What if a Makerspace helps my students make connections to the standards and learn how to control themselves when given the freedom to make their own choices?"

_____

_____

_____

_____

Today's learners need passionate educators. They need educators who know their own strengths and are willing to allow their passions to drive what they do in the classroom every day. Educators who have an intense enthusiasm for what they do each day are the educators who leave the biggest impact on their students. Ask anyone who has gone through the education system, and when they describe the teachers who impacted them the most, they will usually describe a teacher who was passionate about learning, his or her content area, or just life in general. They remember those teachers because passion is contagious and leaves its mark on anyone who comes in contact with it.

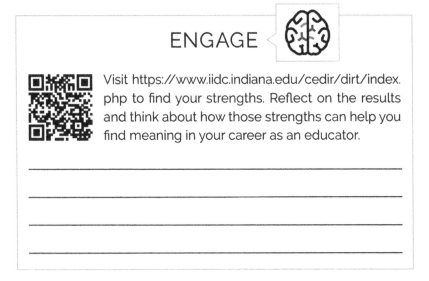

ENGAGE

Visit https://www.iidc.indiana.edu/cedir/dirt/index. php to find your strengths. Reflect on the results and think about how those strengths can help you find meaning in your career as an educator.

Continuing to learn as an educator is imperative and no longer an option for today's teachers. If we stop learning, we stop growing. If we stop growing, we will no longer be able to reach today's learners. They will continue to evolve into learners who do not need the information that we are offering. However, if we choose to learn and grow with them, we will stay relevant and will avoid the very real possibility of becoming obsolete as a profession.

We have made the mistake of assuming that public education is something that will always exist. One of the reasons that we have made this assumption is that there haven't been many other options. Unless parents were willing and had the means to pay for private education, public schools were the only alternative. However, that is changing very quickly. New options for learning are emerging every day, and if we don't make some changes soon, we might find ourselves struggling to find our place.

EMPOWER ⚡

What can you do immediately to learn and grow as an educator? Write down your plan for how you will make this happen starting *today*.

_____

_____

_____

_____

I have spoken with many educators who tell me that they don't want to take the risk to change or even consider "messy" learning as an option in their own classrooms because what they are doing is working. My next question is always, "What do you consider 'working'?" Are we considering compliant students who can regurgitate information on a worksheet or test "working"? Is a system that encourages students to remember rather than reflect really "working"? It's important that we take the time consider what we mean when we say that what we are doing is working.

ENGAGE

Write down your definition of "working." When you say that what you are doing is working in your classroom, what do you mean by that?

_____

_____

_____

_____

As you read through this book, please remember that a mess isn't always a bad thing. I hope to encourage you, as an educator, to embrace messy learning and create a student-driven classroom. In doing so, my hope is that you will find meaning in what you do. And when what you do every day is meaningful, you begin to see purpose and become more intentional about the why behind the learning. Just like growing up, growing as an educator has its uncomfortable stages. It's so important that we push through the hard to get to the amazing. Let's stop making teaching about content and worksheets and start making it about relationships and experiences. Let's embrace the idea of our classrooms being meaningful messes and understand that we are all in this together.

Getting to Know Gen Z

GENERATION Z is unlike anything the education community has seen before. Although it's true that learners have changed throughout the years, never before have we had a generation of learners that had instant access to information. Although all generations have had their own strengths and weaknesses, Gen Z definitely presents more challenges in the traditional classroom than any previous generation. Many of us received information from our parents and teachers, but today's learners can instantly look up facts or the latest news, ask for directions, or even watch a video explaining a particular concept with the click of a button or just by asking Siri.

ENGAGE

Think about this generation of learners. What are some of their strengths? What are some of their weaknesses? Was it easier to identify their strengths or weaknesses?

_____

_____

_____

_____

I have to admit that it drives me crazy that we see so many of Gen Z's strengths as weaknesses in education. So many of the skills that these students will need upon graduation are seen as weaknesses in the traditional school setting. It always amazes me that when asked about this generation's strengths, many of us are only able to come up with a few ideas. When we are asked about their weaknesses, however, it seems that we can go on and on.

Here's the thing: Gen Z was born just like any previous generation. These learners weren't born with the characteristics that we see as their weaknesses. The reality is that they are who they are because of the society in which they have grown up. Instead of complaining about what they can and can't do, it's time to do something. It's time to begin to see today's learners for who they are, recognize what they need from us as educators, and prepare them for what they will need in the future as they leave school.

Perspective has a way of changing everything. Assuming that this generation is unwilling to learn is a mistake. They love to learn. Think about it. Think about how many of your students, or maybe your own children, have taught themselves how to do something by watching a YouTube video. The fact is that they are willing to learn; they are not willing to learn in a way that doesn't represent their world beyond the walls of the classroom. I believe in this generation of learners. I see them for who they are and what they can accomplish. In doing so, my perspective allows me to design meaningful experiences based on what they need rather than what worked for me when I was in the classroom.

I often say that this generation does some very strange things. I will even go so far as to call today's learners "weird." I can say that because I have three of them living in my home. But weird is not always a bad thing. By weird, I mean that they are unusual in a way that is hard for many of us to understand. My daughter

> This generation has given us reason to question the "how," the "what," and, most importantly, the "why" behind the things that we do in the classroom. And guess what . . . it's about time!

prefers to watch someone play with a toy on YouTube rather than playing with it herself. I'm not sure that my boys are even aware that their phones can be used for anything other than sending messages and posting on social media. The only reason we struggle to understand is because they learn so very differently than us and the generations before them. They are not something that we have previously seen in our classrooms. Remember, however, that messy learning shouldn't be easy. This generation is going to question the status quo, push back when expected to simply comply, and create real change because they believe that they can.

Gen Zs have a way of making educators feel uncomfortable. As addressed, they don't learn the way that learners have learned in the past and are lacking many of the skills that previous students didn't have to be taught. I would even argue that if you are super comfortable in education right now, you might be doing it wrong. This generation has given us reason to question the "how," the "what," and, most importantly, the "why" behind the things that we do in the classroom. And guess what . . . it's about time!

REFLECT

What are some things that you see in the classroom from Gen Zs that are weaknesses in the classroom setting but could possibly be strengths in today's society?

_____

_____

_____

_____

_____

_____

_____

_____

_____

_____

Let's look at some things that we know about Gen Zs and how those things impact them as learners. First of all, these are students born from 1995–2014. They have an attention span of 8 seconds and consume on an average of five screens (BCM Partnership, 2015). It's extremely intimidating to even think about educating a learner with an attention span of only 8 seconds. How is that even possible? Many of you might be ready to turn in your resignation based on that fact alone, but just stay with me. The truth is that Gen Z students are able to focus on things that they find meaningful. Unfortunately, much of what we are teaching in the classroom is not meaningful to them.

When they find something meaningless or irrelevant, they're out, they disengage. Sometimes this is demonstrated through misbehavior, apathetic attitudes, or just an unwillingness to engage. Let's dig a little deeper into Gen Z as a generation so that we can find practical ways to engage them as learners in our classrooms.

Gen Z Is All About Right Now

This generation of students tends to enjoy things that are ephemeral. In other words, they like things that last a short time. Take Snapchat, for example. They absolutely love the app because they are able to share instantly and make photos and videos available for others to see for just a short time. They often couldn't care less about saving the images or storing them somewhere. What matters to them is right now.

Gen Z lives in the moment. These learners are all about experiences, what they have to gain from those experiences, and sharing those experiences with others. In doing so, they see themselves as being connected. Being connected gives them instant access to each other's lives and what they are doing at any given moment.

They are not familiar with waiting for anything (Premack, 2018). They are living in a society in which they can instantly order things that they need online, order their food on an app before arriving at a restaurant, and enjoy any music of their choice by simply clicking a button. The fact that many of us had to go to a store to buy toys or had to wait for a song to be played on the radio is completely foreign to them.

This type of environment has created a generation of learners who do not like to wait. They are all about the right now and expect things to happen as instantly as they do in the world around them. I'm not suggesting that we always play into this and never encourage them to wait and practice patience, but I am suggesting that we find ways to use this fact to engage our learners when it is appropriate in the classroom.

Gen Z Wants to Make a Difference in the World

It's not beyond the realm of possibility for [these students] to develop a solution to a problem, share it, and change the world . . .

When I was a student and I created something that I was proud of, I took it home and my parents hung it on the refrigerator. When this generation of learners produces something that they are proud of, they have the opportunity to share it with the world. Because of their instant access to social media, they can connect instantly with anyone at any time. They want to make a difference in the world and believe that they have the power to do so. And guess what? They're right! It's not beyond the realm of possibility for them to develop a solution to a problem, share it, and change the world . . . instantly.

Recently, Alexander Knoll created an app called Ability App (Fryer, 2017). The app makes it possible to search hotels and restaurants to find specific features that are beneficial to those with disabilities. He came up with the idea when he saw a disabled man struggling to open a door. After sharing his idea with *The Ellen DeGeneres Show*, he was invited to be on the show, and the rest is history. This 12-year-old boy who had an idea has changed the lives of so many people simply because he saw a problem and developed a solution. You can learn more about this app by visiting http://www.abilityapp.org.

REFLECT

Do you believe that your learners have ideas that can change the world? How can you give them opportunities to explore and act on those ideas?

_____

_____

_____

_____

_____

_____

Gen Z Is More Entrepreneurial Than Previous Generations

Many of the students sitting in your classroom today do not see themselves working for someone else in the future. Instead, they see themselves owning a business and others working for them. They are more entrepreneurial than previous generations (Beall, 2017). And sometimes, they don't see owning a business as happening in the future; they are making it happen now. Alexander Knoll is a perfect example. Can you imagine being 12 years old and the CEO of your own company? When I was 12 years old, I didn't even know what a CEO was.

Mikaila Ulmer is the founder and CEO of Me & the Bees Lemonade (https://www.meandthebees.com). She is 11 years old and has created a sweetener using honey and flaxseed. She sells her creation at places like Whole Foods and gives back by giving some of her profits to saving honeybees and preventing their extinction.

Nick D'aloisio created Summly (Newnham, 2016). At only 15 years old, he developed an app that summarizes news articles. Yahoo later bought his company for $30 million. Can you even fathom being 15 years old and making that amount of money? I can't wrap my mind around making that amount of money right now!

I could share story after story. Entrepreneurs no longer look like men in suits who have sold their ideas to a large corporation. They look like the kids in your neighborhood sitting around sharing ideas and finding ways to make a difference. They look like the quiet student at the back of the classroom who has a great idea—she can't wait to get home so that she can develop the idea and share it on social media. They look like the student who talks your ear off at recess about an idea that he is so passionate about that he can't help but share.

ENGAGE

Search online for "youth entrepreneurs" and look at the stories and opportunities that exist for today's learners to explore entrepreneurship.

Gen Zs Are Less Driven By Money

As a generation, today's learners aren't necessarily looking for jobs that will result in wealth. Don't get me wrong . . . just like everyone else, they like the idea of having a lot of money. But, more than any generation before them, Gen Zs want to make a difference. Many of them are passionate about creating real change and making an impact on the world around them.

In a recent Undergraduate Awards survey, students were asked "What will motivate you most in choosing a career path upon graduation?" (Hodgson, 2012). I am almost positive that most of my generation would have replied with the amount of money that would be made. But 62% of Gen Z students responded with "ethical values and the potential to make a social impact." The fact is that Gen Z is a powerful generation that has an opportunity and a desire to drive positive change.

REFLECT

Think about the learners in your classroom. Can you see some of them making an impact or creating real change beyond the walls of the classroom?

_____

_____

_____

_____

_____

_____

_____

Gen Z Prefers Instant and Frequent Feedback

Gen Zs are accustomed to receiving feedback. They receive instant feedback from the video games that they play, the coaches of the sports that they play, and the audience that responds to their social media posts that they share from their devices every day. However, in the classroom, we expect them to complete an assignment, wait a week to receive a grade, and have some kind of reaction when they receive that grade. The reality is that this generation prefers feedback over grades. They want to know why they did well or why they didn't do well instead of just receiving a number grade at the top of a paper. We will explore this in more depth later, but it's important to understand that <u>feedback should be given as quickly and as often as possible</u>.

Gen Z is also accustomed to giving feedback. From retail surveys to rating apps, these students are often asked outside of school how they feel about an experience or service that they have received. However, school is different. We give feedback often, but it's possible that we don't ask for their feedback as often as we should. The key to asking for feedback from today's learners is acting on it. They learn very quickly that if they gave feedback and it wasn't used or acted upon, it was a waste of their time. Be genuine in asking them for feedback and doing what you can to use that feedback to make learning more meaningful for them.

Feedback should be given as quickly and as often as possible.

ENGAGE

Think about some ways that you can provide instant or at least more frequent feedback in your classroom. Are you simply returning papers with grades at the top, or are you offering meaningful feedback?

_____

_____

_____

_____

Gen Zs Are Less Collaborative Than Millennials

Research indicates that Gen Zs are less collaborative than Millennials (Goldin, 2017). However, I think when given the opportunity, Gen Zs will not only collaborate but collaborate well. They are well aware of their resources and aren't afraid to reach out for help.

My own kids are the perfect example of this. We went skiing last Christmas, and one of our boys was too old to attend ski school. He had never skied and struggled when it came to stopping. He was great at getting down the mountain, but stopping was not as easy. I took him up the mountain and tried and tried to teach him to stop. I kept telling him he was doing great and encouraged him to just keep trying. Finally, he said, "Mom, let Katy take me up the mountain." Katy is his 10-year-old sister. I explained that I could teach him if he would just listen, but he was not having it.

After lots of persuading, he got on the ski lift with his little sister and up they went. They were on the mountain for a long while, and

I began to get worried. Then, I looked up, and they both came skiing down in perfect form. They got to the bottom, and our son came to a perfect stop! I was so happy for him, but so frustrated that he had not learned from me but from his little sister.

I went over and asked him what in the world she had done (that I had not done) to help him learn how to stop. He said, "She saw me fall down and told me that I looked really silly not being able to stop. She explained that there were lots of people around and if I couldn't figure out how to stop, this was going to be a very embarrassing next few days." Then he said, "So I stopped."

Wow! I had tried every strategy that I knew to help him learn how to do what he needed to be successful. In the end, it didn't matter what I said or did; he needed to learn from someone who was going to tell him like it was.

Our students are no different. We can explain something over and over again. We can give them every strategy that we know of, but they might just need their peers to work with them in a different way. They might need honesty, they might need encouragement, or they might just need to work together until it makes sense. I'm not sure that we make collaboration the priority it should be in education today—and we will talk about this more throughout the book.

REFLECT

Do you give your learners opportunities to experience group work or truly collaborate? What is the difference?

_____

_____

_____

_____

_____

Gen Z Is Less Focused

One of the reasons for Gen Zs' lack of focus is their constant access to media, information, and social interaction (Beall, 2017). Focusing on one thing seems like a waste of time when there are so many things available at any given moment. It's easy to go to the Internet looking for one piece of information and find yourself learning about things that you were never even looking for.

Although they might seem less focused, when Gen Zs are engaged, they are able to focus and do. Think about their focus when it comes to social media. For a generation with an attention span of 8 seconds (BCM Partnership, 2015), Gen Zs are able to spend a great deal of time on Instagram and Snapchat. Why can they spend so much time reading about what their friends are doing but can't focus for more than 8 seconds in our classrooms? Engagement. Relevance. Connections. They are engaged in what they are looking at because it's relevant, and they are able to make meaningful connections.

REFLECT

What does focus look like to you? How do you know when your students are focused?

_____

_____

_____

_____

_____

_____

_____

Gen Z Is Better at Multitasking

Gen Zs don't consume on two screens, and they don't consume on three. This generation consumes on an average of five screens at a time (Patel, 2017). They are very capable of doing more than one thing at a time and prefer to work that way (Beall, 2017). Asking them to sit and listen to someone talk at them for any length of time is asking a lot. It's important to give them opportunities to multitask throughout the day, as sometimes they learn better while doing so.

As I mentioned earlier, these learners weren't born this way. They are the way that they are because of the society that they have grown up in. There are few situations, other than school, that ask them to only focus on one thing at a time. They often play several apps at a time on their devices and are able to quickly check their notifications and still focus on what they were doing before. Although I think there are situations in which students need to learn to focus on one thing and practice being mindful, I think it's important to acknowledge their ability to often do more than one thing at any given time.

REFLECT

How do you feel about your learners multitasking? How would you feel about them doing something other than looking at you while you are talking to the class?

_____

_____

_____

_____

_____

Gen Z Is More Global

Gen Zs don't just simply learn from those immediately around them. They also have global influences and global impact (Beall, 2017). This connectivity makes the world smaller and very accessible. As a generation, they are very connected to the world around them. When I was a kid, I didn't know about what happened in the news unless my parents told me. My parents didn't know until they watched the 10 o'clock news or read the newspaper the next morning. This is no longer the case. We now know instantly what is happening all over the world all of the time, and so do our students.

Although previous generations had pen pals whom we would write letters to and wait weeks for a response, today's learners can video chat instantly with anyone at anytime, anywhere in the world. They can send an e-mail, text message, or direct message and receive a response in seconds or minutes. They are not limited by the space that they are in. In other words, they are able to connect well beyond the walls of the classroom, with others all over the world.

REFLECT

What can you do to make global learning a priority in your classroom? How can you connect your classroom?

_____

_____

_____

_____

This generation of learners can change the world. Sure, they are very different and have many qualities that are unlike anything that we've seen before. However, we must stop seeing these perceived weaknesses as such and realize that many of these "weaknesses" are the very tools that will allow learners to change the world. That being said, we need to develop those skills and not discourage these students because they make us uncomfortable.

Giving Students What They Deserve

THERE are certain things that every student deserves through-out his or her learning journey. Although there are specific things that students need, specific standards that must be taught, and specific services that students must receive, the bottom line is that there are certain opportunities that all learners *deserve* from their school experience.

An opportunity simply means that we make it possible for students to do something. In this case, I believe that there are certain opportunities that make it possible for this generation to experience real learning. Real learning is learning that is meaningful, relevant, and results in an experience that takes students' learning beyond surface level. Table 1 describes several differences between surface-level learning and real learning.

Surface-level learning results in being able to pass a test that is given fairly soon after the learning has taken place. Students are simply able to regurgitate what they were told, or they are able to use

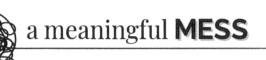

Table 1
Surface-Level Learning Versus Real Learning

Surface-Level Learning	Real Learning
Learner is able to . . .	Learner is able to . . .
Regurgitate facts/information	Understand the why
Complete worksheets	Apply learning in any situation
Consume what is being taught	Produce based on what was learned

strategies that they practiced over and over again as long as the problem is fairly similar to the examples that they were given in class. The problem with this type of learning is the lack of true understanding. And, unfortunately, if we aren't giving students opportunities to experience this real learning, we are setting them up to have unrealistic expectations of what learning will look like in the future when deep understanding is necessary to move forward.

> Real learning is learning that is meaningful, relevant, and results in an experience that takes students' learning beyond surface level.

Think about the difference between snorkeling and scuba diving. Although both allow you to experience being beneath the water, snorkeling requires you to stay at surface level. Because of this, those who snorkel are limited in what they can experience. They can only see and experience what is right beneath them, and they are limited by the need to stay close to the surface. They might be able to take some brief dives, but they can't go too far. Scuba divers, however, have the freedom to truly explore and experience what is beneath the surface. They have more room to spread out and experience the ocean in order see things that simply can't be seen from the surface level.

I'm not suggesting that every learner is ready to go scuba diving. We have many learners who need to stay at the surface while they prepare to be able to dive deeper in the future. In fact, I often say that differentiation doesn't mean that everyone gets a different experience. It means that students experience learning differently. In other words, if I was traveling with friends and had never been beneath the ocean, I would need to snorkel before learning to scuba dive. The same is true for many of our learners. They may need a few more tools, more confidence, or more support before they head for deeper waters. But what if you had been scuba diving for years and then were put into a situation in which you had to snorkel because the rest of the group wasn't ready to go deeper? You have all of your gear, all of the necessary training, and plenty of confidence to explore the waters below, but you are not able to do so because everyone else is learning the basics. I think we can all agree that this would not be a fun situation.

The same is true for many of our gifted learners or any learner who has shown mastery and is ready to move into deeper learning and explore independently. Although it may seem safer and easier to stay at the surface, the real experience (and fun) happens when divers take the risk to go deep and explore.

EMPOWER ⚡

Think about a learning experience that you have coming up soon. How will you engage your learners who need to snorkel and stay at the surface, and how will you engage your learners who are ready to scuba dive and go deeper?

_____

_____

_____

_____

_____

Core Beliefs

As educators, many of us have a philosophy of education. In fact, we've had to share that philosophy in job interviews, with parents, and with administrators. I wonder how often we truly reflect on that philosophy and consider the why that drives what we say that we believe. In order to do so, it's important to go beyond the philosophy and identify your core beliefs. You see, your core beliefs about education, students, learning, and relationships are already impacting what you do and how you teach. They are your "why," the reason that you do what you do. But have you ever taken time to identify those core beliefs?

> Core beliefs enable educators to stay focused and hold their position, regardless of the situation.

As I began to take risks and do things differently in my own classroom, I began to realize that my philosophy of education just wasn't enough. It wasn't until later in my career that I realized I needed to anchor my teaching by creating a core belief system. Just as an anchor keeps a ship from drifting because of wind and current, core beliefs enable educators to stay focused and hold their position, regardless of the situation.

My core beliefs were identified over time. Some of them were realized by something that happened in the classroom, others were identified as I learned from others in education, and some had been there all along, I just hadn't taken the time to make them a priority in my classroom. If I'm completely honest, a couple of my core beliefs exist because of what I want my own children to experience in education. Let me share them with you as you begin to think about your own core beliefs.

My core beliefs are (McNair, 2018):

1. I believe that every student deserves an opportunity to experience new learning.
2. I believe that every student deserves an opportunity to learn by doing.
3. I believe that every student deserves an opportunity to learn from failure.
4. I believe that every student deserves an opportunity to share their learning.
5. I believe that every student deserves an opportunity to pursue their passions during the school day.

Core Belief #1: Opportunities to Experience New Learning

Being at school and sitting in a traditional classroom is hard enough for this generation of learners. It's easy to imagine how much harder it might be if you already know what is being taught. Think about yourself as you sit in a meeting in which information is being given that (a) doesn't apply to you or (b) could have been sent in an e-mail. The reality is that as adults in this situation, we feel frustrated and angry . . . we feel like our time is being wasted.

Why do we expect students to react any differently? I know how hard this is for me, and I only have to do it maybe once or twice a month. Whether it's a professional development that is not relevant to my job or a technology workshop in which the speakers are explaining things that I already understand, it is equally difficult to sit through. I find myself thinking of all of the things that I could be doing and how I will never be able to get that time back. I can't imagine how difficult this must be for learners who experience this 5 days a week, 7 hours a day.

How do we know if we are giving our students opportunities to experience new learning? First and foremost, we must know our students well. Watch their body language, ask questions, and check for understanding before you assume that a learning experience is new content to everyone in the classroom. These strategies can provide you with new perspectives that you might not see if you don't make them priorities. I can think of many days in my classroom that I just came in, taught the lesson, and checked for understanding. Unfortunately, I sometimes missed opportunities to really get to know my learners because I was so focused on getting through the content.

You might be wondering, "What will my students who have already mastered what I'm teaching do in order to experience new learning while I am teaching the rest of the class?" There are so many options:

- Give them an opportunity to learn a new language using Duolingo (https://www.duolingo.com).
- Encourage them to experience critical thinking by watching a TED Talk and reflecting on what they have learned.
- Let them explore current events using DogoNews (https://www.dogonews.com) or Newsela (https://newsela.com).
- Encourage them to learn something new on Wonderopolis by searching their own interests or reading the Wonder of the Day (https://www.wonderopolis.org).
- Give them an opportunity to learn to play chess. ChessKid (https://www.chesskid.com) is the curriculum that I used in my own classroom as we learned together how to play the game.

The possibilities are endless. Just don't ask students to sit through something that they already know and be compliant just for the sake of playing the game.

EMPOWER ⚡

Can you think of some of your learners who are not experiencing new learning every day? What is something that you can do tomorrow to ensure that they are able to do so?

_____

_____

_____

_____

_____

_____

_____

_____

_____

Core Belief #2: Opportunities to Learn by Doing

Learning should not happen to someone. It should be experienced, and our students should be active participants rather than passive receivers of knowledge. Active means to be engaged in a particular activity. Engagement and compliance look different, and as we will discuss later in this book, it is through engagement and empowerment that students are able to experience real learning.

This generation of students learns by doing (Kozinsky, 2017). Application is important as they learn. Only through application can learners truly understand what is being addressed. Think about this: If students are only learning a specific concept through repetitive practice or by completing worksheets, are they really showing that they understand, or are they simply proving that they can listen and do what they are told? Is that what we are striving for?

As educators, we must realize that the more students are able to do, the deeper they move beyond surface-level learning. And chances are, if they can apply a standard in a real situation, they will be able to answer questions about that same standard on a worksheet, test, or anything else that is put in front them because they truly understand the concept.

There are so many ways that our students can learn by doing:

- Provide them with a real problem and ask them to solve it using the standards that were addressed that week.
- Allow them to learn by pursuing their passion or impacting change in their school, community, or even the world.
- Ask them to explore real learning by creating something to show their learning, as they move away from simply consuming and toward producing.
- Ask them to create a website, using Weebly for Education, about what is being learned to share with the rest of the class . . . or the rest of the world!
- Encourage them to code a video game for the rest of the class to play about what is being learned.

Core Belief #3: Opportunities to Learn From Failure

Every student deserves an opportunity to see failure for what it is. In and of itself, failure is not a negative thing. However, when not seen as an opportunity to learn and grow, failure gets in the way of real learning. I am convinced that sometimes the best learning happens in the struggle. If students are not given the opportunity to learn and grow from failure, they miss out on valuable learning. Table 2 includes a list of ways failure is often perceived in school compared to how failure should be perceived in real life.

Failure is not a word that we should use to describe a student, and it's not a word that students should ever associate with themselves.

Table 2

Perception of Failure in School Versus Real Life

Failure in School	Failure in Real Life
A result of not doing something	A result of taking a risk
Given in the form of a grade	Given in the form of feedback
End result	Just the beginning
Negative experience	Opportunity to learn and grow

Failure is something that is experienced, something that happens. Students are never failures. They may experience failure, learn from failure, and grow from failure, but they should never be defined by failure. Let's start calling failure what it is and encouraging our learners to do the same . . . failure is an opportunity to learn and grow.

When learners are given real opportunities to fail and struggle, they become comfortable having to figure things out on their own. Most state assessments do not allow educators to help students as they take the test. We simply have to tell them on test day that we can't help them and that they need to do their best. If that is not something that they have heard all year long, this can make students very uncomfortable.

If throughout the school year we have answered questions, guided students toward the correct answer, and kept them from struggling, we are actually preparing them for a future of frustration and entitlement. However, giving them opportunities to fail, push past the struggle, and learn from that experience provides students with the confidence that they will need moving forward.

> Failure is an opportunity to learn and grow.

ENGAGE

How would you define *failure*? How would you define *failing*? Are they the same thing, and how can you help your learners understand the difference?

_____

_____

_____

_____

Core Belief #4: Opportunities to Share Learning

Authentic audiences play an important role in the learning experience. When sharing their work with an audience, students have a reason to invest and create work that represents them well. Keeping work inside the four walls of the classroom sends the message that the teacher's opinion of the work is the only one that matters. Sharing work, however, gives learners an opportunity to see social media as a way to promote themselves positively. Digital citizenship shouldn't simply address what students shouldn't be doing online. Let's start helping them recognize and understand what they can do and should do to create a digital footprint that will serve them well for years to come.

This generation of learners is comfortable with sharing on a large scale. They don't typically produce content and media at home that isn't shared with an authentic audience. We know that Gen Zs are very comfortable learning alongside other students (Kozinsky, 2017). Whether that happens online or in-person makes no difference to them. They know that they can go online to experience learning or share their own learning from anywhere at any time.

There are many ways to encourage learners to produce for an authentic audience. Many teachers have students write books. Sometimes, those books are even published by using websites and apps like StoryJumper (https://www.storyjumper.com) or Book Creator. Unfortunately, we often just send those published books home with the students for their parents and family to read. As a writer, I can tell you that if my parents and family were the ones reading my book, I'd be pretty disappointed and frustrated that I took the time to write and share my story. Although I love that they get copies and they are very proud, the reality is that without an audience, my writing loses its purpose. Why is publishing a work at school any different? Share students' work with others by doing any of the following:

- Put their book in the school library where other students can check it out.
- Allow them to create a website about what they have learned that can be shared with the world.
- Give them opportunities to share their learning on social media. (*Note.* Several safety recommendations for sharing student work online are shared in Chapter 10.)

REFLECT

How comfortable are you with students sharing work? Do you share your own work? Why or why not?

_____

_____

_____

_____

_____

The truth is that when students know their work is going to be shared with an authentic audience, they become more intentional. They think about what they are doing and are cognizant of the fact that it isn't simply for their teacher or even their class, but for the world. They take pride in what they post online because they get it . . . they know the potential is there for someone to see their work or their ideas. It's not about being compliant and doing it because they have to. When they are producing for an audience, there is purpose and reason behind the work.

For students who are too young to share their work on social media, it can be shared for them or you can use a platform like GoBubble, a safe social media platform for learners under 13. It is free for educators and gives you an opportunity to control who your learners are connected with. You can choose to allow your students to connect amongst themselves, or with parents and even other classrooms around the world. GoBubble is monitored very closely, and the content is moderated.

Core Belief #5: Opportunities to Pursue Passions During the School Day

We all have passions and interests. When we hear those passions addressed or brought up in conversation, we become more engaged, more willing to hear what is being shared. Students are no different. If we can find a way to tap into their passions while giving them opportunities to learn the standards, the classroom becomes a different place. Instead of being a place where they are expected to listen to someone talk and hope that they can somehow make a connection, they are given the opportunity to purposefully make connections to what is being learned through their own interests, passions, and goals. I believe that every single student has a passion and can learn through that passion. They simply need us, as educators, to allow them to do so.

Genius Hour is such a wonderful way for students to not only explore their passions, but also create, make, and design a product to be shared with an audience. In providing time during the school day for students to do this, educators help students see learning differently. Later in the book, I will provide more detail about Genius Hour and what it can look like in the classroom.

Identifying Your Core Beliefs

Identifying your core beliefs and sharing them with others can help to make them a reality. So, how do you know what they are? How can you share them, and why should they be a top priority? I think it's best to start with what you believe that every student deserves. I like to think of my core beliefs as targets to aim for with every learning experience that is designed, every tool that is used, and every relationship that is being built. Don't get me wrong, there have been many times when I have missed the mark. But when that happened, I simply acknowledged it, regained focus, and aimed more carefully with the next attempt.

> Identifying, activating, and sharing your core beliefs will keep you accountable to what you believe to be true.

My five core beliefs began to drive everything that I did in the classroom and still today drive everything that I share. Because I believe these things, I am passionate about real learning experiences like Genius Hour and Makerspace. I will talk to anyone who will listen about my experience with my own students and how allowing them to own their learning by pursuing their passions changed everything.

Oftentimes, we have great ideas and ambitions when the school year starts. Then, things get crazy and we revert back to what's easy, what's comfortable, and what's familiar. For me, having these core beliefs held me accountable as I took risks and tried new things. I knew that if a risk was going to result in one of these beliefs being activated, it was probably a good idea, even if it wasn't successful right away.

Now, it's your turn. What do you believe all learners deserve? And if they truly deserve it, isn't it imperative that we make those things a priority in our classrooms regardless of time, lack of resources, and other obstacles that simply become excuses if we don't find ways around them?

Take some time to think about this. Start with something as simple as "I believe . . ." and then be completely honest. Don't get caught up in worrying about what others will think about your core beliefs or if you will be able to make them happen. Just focus on what you honestly believe that all students deserve.

EMPOWER

Below are some simple steps that you can take to not only identify, but also activate and share your core beliefs.

1. Take some time to focus on what you believe to be true about education.
2. Write down 3–5 of those beliefs that you think deserve your focus and attention.
3. Think about the ways that your beliefs can be activated. In other words, how can you make them happen?
4. Post your core beliefs in a place where you will see them every single day.
5. Share your beliefs on Twitter using #ameaningfulmess and with anyone else who will listen.

_____

_____

_____

_____

The reality is that although you are accountable to lots of people, your ultimate accountability is to the learners who are relying on you to create meaningful experiences that will engage and empower. Identifying, activating, and sharing your core beliefs will keep you accountable to what you believe to be true. They will serve as an anchor when the waters get rough or the winds begin to blow. Instead of being moved, your core beliefs will give you the foundation that you need to make decisions based on what is best for your learners.

Building Upon Your Core Beliefs

Your core beliefs should give your students opportunities to be to be empowered. We will look closely at empowerment later in this book, but it is only through empowerment that students will begin to own their learning in a way that surpasses simply doing what is expected or what is required. Instead, they begin to really understand why they are learning and the impact that learning will have on them and their future.

As educators, we owe it to our students to expect more than compliance. It's time to raise the bar and empower our students to go deep. In doing so, they will experience more than we might have even expected. Chances are that they will surprise us with their willingness to create, learn, and explore if we can just let go of some of the control and put the ball in their court.

Giving today's learners these opportunities encourages them to push beyond what is safe and easy, as they take risks to go beyond the limitations that we have placed upon them and they have placed upon themselves. In doing so, they will begin to make connections, deepen their understanding, and become empowered as learners that know what real learning looks like.

Let's talk about video games. I hear so many educators say that if we could just get students to pay as much attention in the classroom as they do to their video games, things would be just fine. Well, what is it about video games that causes today's learners to play for hours and hours? Why will they take risks and continue to play even when they are not successful most of the time?

There are three reasons that kids will spend every waking hour gaming, even when they are not successful:

1. **They are given the opportunity to fail safely.** What does it look like to fail safely? When failure is experienced on a video game, nothing happens. Players are just given the opportunity to try again and again and again. They don't have to answer to anyone or explain themselves, and no one is disappointed in them. They just keep trying until they get it right.

2. **Video games give players instant feedback.** Players know instantly what they did wrong and what they can do differently to reach a better outcome. That's completely different than what we do in education. Oftentimes, students simply receive a grade and no feedback on what they could've done differently to be more successful. If feedback is given, it is not often immediate.

3. **Leveling up is probably the main reason that so many gamers enjoy playing.** They don't have to wait on anyone else to get something done before they are able to level up. They simply master a specific level, and they are instantly given the opportunity to move on to a more challenging level. This opportunity to reach a more challenging level drives them to continue pushing themselves toward their ultimate goal, conquering the entire game.

How can we take some of these attributes of video games and make them a reality in the classroom? It's not as hard as it might sound. Build upon your core beliefs with these principles. Begin by allowing students to fail safely. Give them opportunities to fail without consequences as long as they learn and grow from that failure. Stop making failure about grades, and instead, make it about a desire to become better. Give opportunities to make up lower grades and retake tests. In doing so, you send the message to your students that failure is about learning. When we shut our students down and refuse to give opportunities to learn and grow, we begin to help them form an unrealistic view of what failure is and what it looks like in the real world.

Many of our learners have growth mindsets when it comes to things that they do outside of school. Video games, in particular, require players to be willing to learn new things, work through frustration, challenge themselves, and persist in spite of the obstacles that come their way. In the classroom, however, our students may have fixed mindsets and are not willing to do many of these things. This is often because they are not put in situations during their school day that truly encourage a growth mindset. Students can't grow if they are not given real opportunities to improve or work on the areas in which they need growth.

> Stop making failure about grades, and instead, make it about a desire to become better.

Give your learners instant feedback. Use tools like Flipgrid and Kidblog to hear their voices and respond. Flipgrid is a video response tool that gives you as the educator an opportunity to give feedback. Kidblog is a blogging platform that allows students to write and publish blog posts. Instant feedback can be received from the classroom, the teacher, and even the world. Allow their peers to respond, and ultimately, share their work with the world so that the feedback is received from an authentic audience. Instant feedback helps students know what improvements need to be made while they still care.

Finally, offer opportunities to "level up." Remember, we talked about how every student deserves the opportunity to experience new learning. How can this happen if students can't level up when they have mastered what is being focused on in the classroom? Being able to level up gives many learners a reason to want to be in the classroom. If, however, they can't level up and they simply have to sit and listen to things that they already know, why would they want to be there? There is no reason for them to work harder and achieve more because nothing will happen if they do. They will still be sitting in a desk, waiting for their peers to catch up with them, so that they can possibly move on to something that is challenging or new to them as a learner.

ENGAGE

How can you make these three things a priority in your classroom? How can you allow your learners to fail safely, receive instant feedback, and level up?

_____

_____

_____

_____

Letting Go of Control

OUR eldest is just learning to drive. He is just a couple of months away from getting his license, and I am a nervous wreck. When we first started allowing him to drive after getting his permit, it was so much harder than I ever imagined. I was so nervous, so afraid that he would do something wrong and, ultimately, cause an accident or be involved in an accident caused by someone else.

It has been so hard to just let him drive and offer suggestions in a calm manner. As we began this learning experience, I found myself making the entire driving situation a lot harder than it needed to be. In doing so, I made him nervous and even fearful about doing something that I knew he was going to be doing on his own in a very short amount of time.

One day, I allowed him to drive me into town, and I decided I was just going to relax. I sat back, trusted that he had been prepared, and I just let him go. And guess what? He did great! He had become a great driver who used just enough precaution to be safe but not so much that he was a danger to others. I remember looking over at him in the driver's seat and realizing how fast time had flown by and how so many things had brought us to this moment, the moment that he was actually driving me and I was just there to offer advice and guidance if he needed me.

Here's the thing . . . he did ask questions when it was necessary. He would ask about right of way, what to do when the flow of traffic is greater than the speed limit, and other questions that he would have never asked if I had continued to instruct him on every little thing. Instead, he would have just assumed that I had told him everything and wouldn't want to ask any questions because that would just mean more advice and more talking.

I think the shift to a student-driven classroom is very similar to this situation. We tend to want to help students too often and give too much of our own advice throughout the day in a teacher-driven situation. We don't do this because we are control freaks (well, maybe sometimes). We just want them to be successful. We want to help them, guide them, and give them the advice they need to continue to move forward and grow as learners.

But the problem is this . . . in doing so, we are creating learners who expect to be spoon-fed, can't do things independently, and never ask the questions they really need to ask to experience that real learning that we talked about in the previous chapter. Instead, they just assume that if it's something they need to know, we would have told them because we have always done so.

Rethinking Classroom Rules and Teacher Control

Letting go of control can be very difficult. George S. Patton said, "Don't tell people how to do things, tell them what to do and let them surprise you with their results." I think this is an easy way to begin to let go of some of the control that we feel like we must have as educators. Tell students what you need from them, and let them figure out how to make that happen.

A perfect example of this is classroom rules. In many classrooms, there are several rules. Rule #1 is usually not to talk while the teacher is talking. Rule #2 might be for students to keep their hands, feet, and objects to themselves, and Rule #3 might be for students to raise their hands before speaking. What if every classroom only had one rule? What if that rule was simply to be respectful? In having just this one rule, we are telling our students what we expect and what we need them to do. Is it necessary to be as specific as breaking it down into five, sometimes as many as 10, rules?

> What if every classroom only had one rule? What if that rule was simply to be respectful?

By having one rule, you build trust by helping your students understand that you trust them enough to know what respect looks like. If your students aren't sure what respect means, much less what it looks like, then have a conversation and discuss what you expect, model what respect is and have discussions about what it is not. By giving a list of rules and making it about compliance, you send a negative message to your learners from day one. And they hear that message loud and clear . . . "I don't trust you enough to figure out what it means to make good choices and respect each other, so I am going to be super specific so that I can have more control over certain situations."

I also believe that making this rule a priority helps our learners find ways to practice respect. As educators it is so important that we help them understand that you don't have to agree with someone, look like someone, or think like someone in order to respect someone. Instead, respect is a choice that we make. In choosing to be respectful, we choose what's right and what will result in relationships that are real and meaningful. When we don't choose respect, we are choosing selfishness and destruction of another person. Respect is not something that we can choose to not to address in our classrooms. Today's learners need to not only see, but also experience respect so that they can create real change outside of the classroom by demonstrating the respect that they've learned inside the classroom.

EMPOWER ⚡

What do your classroom rules look like? How can you tweak them to show your learners that you trust them?

_____

_____

_____

_____

I know from experience that when students drive the learning, they become more curious, begin to ask more questions, and oftentimes will surprise you with their willingness and ability to figure things out. So many of the things that we feel like we need to tell them are actually things that they already know or will find out if we will just create the right experiences. In other words, we waste a lot of time giving details and sharing information that they do not need.

Just like my son, today's learners will know when they need to ask and will sometimes begin to ask about things that would have never been addressed if we were giving them all of the answers. Sometimes hearing their perspective and seeing the learning from that perspective changes everything.

I absolutely love Alice Keeler's quote, "Would you want to be a learner in your own classroom?" I can think of many years in my teaching career when, sadly, my answer would have been "No." Although I always tried to be the best teacher that I could be, I oftentimes tried to control every student, every situation, and even every strategy that they used to create solutions.

REFLECT

Would you want to be a learner in your own classroom? If not, what would you change so that you would feel differently?

_____

_____

_____

_____

I know what you are thinking . . . "When I give my students more control, they are unwilling to take initiative." Or, "If I really let my students drive the learning, we will never get anywhere." Although this might be the case in the beginning, it won't be for long. Of course, when you begin to give them some control, they will not know what to do or how to react. They will feel as if you are not doing your job and expecting too much of them. They will be frustrated and anxious.

They will be in uncharted waters, unfamiliar territory. Rather than having you as their instructor and giver of information, you have become their facilitator and asker of questions. Think about children when it's time to give up their safety blankets or pacifiers. They definitely aren't happy in the beginning, but they begin to find ways to move past the need for constant comfort and realize that they are fully capable of living life without whatever it was that they were tethered to.

I recently read that more than 80% of the ocean is undiscovered (National Ocean and Atmospheric Administration, 2018). That means that if someone doesn't go into uncharted waters, we will have only learned what we could've learned from the less than 20% that has been discovered. Can you imagine what is still out there to be discovered? There are amazing creatures, plant life, and underwater mysteries waiting to be found, and yet, we are still so far away from seeing what lies beneath.

There are many reasons that percentage is so high. It involves risk, time, and patience to explore the depths of the oceans. Similarly, it involves risk, time, and patience to allow students to drive their learning. We may only be scratching the surface of what our students are able to do. By letting them drive, we might be able to explore and learn more than ever before. We might begin to realize that we had only given them an opportunity to explore 5%, and that 95% is being left unexplored because of our own fears and expectations of what school is supposed to look like.

EMPOWER ⚡

What percentage of your students' learning would you predict is undiscovered? How can you help them explore uncharted waters when it comes to their learning?

_____

_____

_____

_____

Moving Toward Student-Driven Learning

Student-driven learning looks very different than teacher-driven learning. It's not easy, it's messy, and it requires a two-way trust that creates a culture of learning instead of teaching. So what is the difference, and what does student-driven learning look like in the classroom? How do we move past doing what we've always done and what we know well into this territory that is very risky and even a little uncomfortable for many of us?

We start by giving the classroom back to our students. Stop calling it "my classroom" and begin to call it theirs. I can remember the day that I decided to make this small change in my own classroom. I actually gave up my teacher desk and began to sit out among my students. I was no longer tethered to my computer, as I just used a laptop and did what I needed to do from a student desk.

There was nothing in the room that was off limits for them. I created a space that was truly theirs and that we all used to learn and grow in whatever ways were most meaningful each day. I'm not going to lie . . . I was really nervous at first. We had received a grant for new flexible seating, and I allowed my students to give input on what they wanted from their learning environment. I thought, "What am I doing? This is my classroom, and I want my students to respect it as such." But I also knew that if I wanted them to take ownership of their learning, I needed to give my students ownership of the space. I had to walk the walk instead of just talking the talk. It was time to put my money where my mouth was and start showing my students that I was serious about giving them the freedom to own their learning.

Although there wasn't an instant, earth-shattering change overnight, my classroom's culture did begin to change over time. My learners began to realize that I trusted them enough to give them more freedom

> A student-driven classroom involves learners really taking control and driving their learning.

and more ownership. In doing so, I sent the message loud and clear that I had high expectations. And I began to notice small things, like they began taking better care of our equipment. By sitting out among them, I was able to hear conversations that gave me an opportunity to weave more learning into their classroom experiences. They no longer had to raise their hands and announce to the class that they didn't understand. I was able to see instantly who was ready to move on and who needed extra help. They took more pride in the classroom and began cleaning up without being asked. In giving them ownership of the classroom, it was no longer about compliance and doing things because I told them to. It was about empowerment, and they began to do things because we had shifted the ownership and created a culture of community.

EMPOWER ⚡

What can you do to help your learners feel ownership in the classroom? Could you go deskless? How would you feel about sitting among your learners rather than having your own space?

_____

_____

_____

_____

_____

_____

_____

Letting Students D.R.I.V.E.

Student-centered and student-driven are two very similar but also different ways for students to experience learning. Student-centered learning can still be driven by the teacher. It's definitely focused on what individual students need and want in the classroom, but it doesn't give the learners as much control as a student-driven classroom. A student-driven classroom involves learners really taking control and driving their learning. The teacher is in the passenger seat, guiding and facilitating when he or she is needed. Letting our learners D.R.I.V.E. impacts learning in a powerful way:

- D: Determination
- R: Relevance
- I: Independence
- V: Value
- E: Empowerment

Determination

When students D.R.I.V.E. the learning, amazing things begin to happen. For starters, they are often determined to prove that they can learn on their own terms. Although they may be uncomfortable at first, when the concept of real student-driven learning takes hold in the classroom, determination begins to set in. Students become determined to find their own way, determined to push through difficult situations, and determined to prove that they can be trusted to take their learning to the next level.

Students also become determined to learn things that they could not have cared less about when they were being taught by the teacher. They want to prove that when given the opportunity, they can and will learn. They want us to see that when we make a way for real learning to happen, they will walk through that door. Although some students may be hesitant at first and will push back when given the freedom, they will eventually realize that with determination and a willingness to learn, their ownership of the learning has the potential to change everything.

Relevance

Relevance is something that must be present in order for this generation to make connections with what is being learned. If the content is not relevant to them and their world right now, it is difficult for them to understand why there is a reason to learn. If connections aren't made between what is being learned and how it applies to them, they simply don't understand why we are wasting their time. I often say that we must connect to students' "right now." Stating that they will need to know something later just makes them wonder why they can't just YouTube or Google it later when it is needed. However, connecting to their "right now" gives them a reason to invest. Relevance is the reason behind the learning. There is nothing wrong with a student asking, "Why do I need to know this?" In fact, students should be asking this question, and, as educators, we should be able to give them an answer.

When students drive the learning, they begin to find the relevance. They will no longer need to ask why they need to know something because it will be very clear as they begin to make important connections. It's a good idea to ask students to make connections before they leave the classroom every day. Ask them to share what connections they made and what was relevant to them after the experience. This generation is very familiar with streaks. They often keep streaks going with their friends on social media as a challenge to stay connected. It might even be a good idea to see how long they can keep a streak alive regarding the connections that they make to the content. Let me explain. Challenge students every day to find a way to connect the content that was learned beyond the walls of the classroom. When they come in the next the day, if they can explain that connection, their streak stays alive. The first time that they can't make a connection, their streak starts over. When they intentionally make these connections, it becomes easier to know the why behind what is being learned, giving them a different and very important perspective.

EMPOWER ⚡

What are some ways that you can encourage your learners to find relevance in something that they will be learning this week?

_____

_____

_____

_____

Independence

Being independent at school is uncomfortable for this generation. They know how to play the school game. They know that, based on what they know of school right now, they come in and are told what to do, how to do it, and when to do it. Making decisions and being independent are not things that they associate with school.

Therefore, they have become dependent on us as educators to solve problems and make decisions for them throughout the day.

As I have said, the best learning happens in the struggle. I rarely learn from situations that come easily, but I learn a ton from things that go wrong. Our students need to experience that struggle so that they are able to be independent. As teachers, we typically feel the need to guide, give answers, and make suggestions so that we feel successful as educators. The truth is that when our students don't know the answers, we feel anxious and even blame ourselves. It's time to put the learning in their court. Give them real experiences that will cause struggle, frustration, and, as we discussed earlier, even failure. In doing so, you are reminding your students, of all ability levels, that they can learn through the struggle. For gifted students, I think that it's also important to remember that being gifted doesn't mean a student won't struggle, and experiencing struggle doesn't mean a student isn't gifted.

Please know that I'm not encouraging you as an educator to kick your feet up, drink a Coke, sit back, and watch your students struggle without offering encouragement and advice. Instead, I'm simply suggesting that we look for opportunities to allow struggle to create a level of independence that won't be reached if students are dependent on the teacher for every decision that they make throughout the school day.

My own kids are very capable of doing many things. If, however, I'm going to do something for them, they will certainly let me. Think about a baby when he or she is learning to eat. The baby is just fine being spoon-fed, but at some point, we have to be willing to let him or her learn. When children begin to feed themselves, it's a complete mess. They often get more food on their clothes and the floor than they do in their mouths. But then something happens . . . they begin to hold the spoon in a more natural fashion. They know where to put the food in order for it to be most beneficial to them. They begin to figure it out!

The same is true for messy learning. When we first provide students with the independence that they need to experience real learning, they are going to make mistakes. They will miss some learning opportunities, and sometimes it will seem as though independent learning is too far out of their reach. But then something happens . . . they begin know how to handle the learning. They know what to do with what is learned so that it is most beneficial for them. They begin to figure it out!

When given the opportunity to be independent and make choices, today's learners will often surprise those around them. Although they seem to be completely dependent, there is a part of them just waiting for someone to ask them what they think, how they feel, or how they learn. I can honestly say that when I took time to really know my students as learners, I was amazed at how different they were as individual learners. It's easy to see them as a class, a group of learners, or a grade level. But the reality is that they are all individuals who deserve the opportunity to practice independence while at school.

EMPOWER ⚡

Do you see your learners as independent? What are some things that you do right now to spoon-feed them that can be eliminated as you encourage them to become independent learners?

_____

_____

_____

_____

_____

_____

Value

There are many things in life that I value. I value time with family, time with friends, pursuing change in education, and spending time talking to educators who are passionate about doing what is best for this generation of learners. Because I value these things, I make time for them. I carve out time in my day and pursue opportunities that will allow me time to make these things happen.

Similar things happen when our learners value what is being learned. When they drive the learning, they often find value, and that value gives them a desire to pursue whatever it is that is being learned. Just like a customer has to find value in what is being purchased, learners have to find value in what is being learned. If they can't find that value, they will become disinterested and disconnected, resulting in apathy, noncompliance, or maybe even behavior issues. And just like a customer who doesn't find value in a product and leaves it on the shelf, our students will walk out of our classrooms and leave the learning behind.

REFLECT

What are some things that you value? How do you know they are valuable to you?

_____

_____

_____

_____

_____

_____

_____

Empowerment

Finally, empowerment naturally happens in the student-driven classroom. This empowerment changes the culture of a classroom. It's no longer about rules, checklists, and lesson plans. Instead, it's about students being driven by their own desire to learn. It's very common for educators to focus on engaging students during a learning experience. But, have you thought about how you can empower them? What can be done to make learning about the connections that students make? Empowered learners can't help but want to drive the learning. Engaged learners are like young drivers with a permit. They expect someone else to tell them what to do and how to do it, while making it fun and engaging. Empowered learners have their license and are ready to go! They don't need someone encouraging them to learn. Instead, they have been empowered to get into the driver's seat and take off.

You will hear this word a lot throughout this book, as I believe empowerment is one of the things that we are missing in today's classrooms. When today's students become empowered, they begin to realize who they are as learners, and this enables them to truly D.R.I.V.E. the learning in a way that will create a culture of real learning.

> Empowerment naturally happens in the student-driven classroom.

REFLECT

What does the word *empowerment* mean to you?

_____

_____

Student-driven learning can be messy. It will feel out of control, and you might feel just like I did so often as my son was driving me around. I wanted to grab the wheel, offer constant advice, and control his every move. But if I had done those things, he would not have been prepared to drive on his own. I would never have trusted him to drive on his own when he finally did receive his license. But because I gave him real opportunities to be in control of the situation, he was more than prepared to drive safely and independently even when I wasn't in the car. Just like the time came when I wasn't going to be with my son, the time will come when you will not be with your learners. So, let's make it a priority to let them D.R.I.V.E. in order to experience learning in a way that is most meaningful and will impact them well beyond the school year that they have with us in the classroom.

ENGAGE

Which aspect of student-driven learning seems most rewarding or exciting for you as an educator? Why?

_____

_____

_____

_____

Empowerment Versus Compliance

WHEN I remember myself as a learner, I remember sitting in a desk, listening to my teacher talk and wishing I was anywhere in the world but sitting in that place at that moment in time. I remember wondering why I needed to know what my teacher was talking about, wondering how I was going ever going to use algebra in my life after school, and watching the minutes tick by as I thought of all of the other things I could have been doing.

However, I was compliant. I rarely got in trouble, typically did my work, and played the game of school well. At first glance, my teachers probably assumed that I was engaged and enjoyed being at school. But in many of my classes, I wasn't really learning. I was listening, I was remembering, and then I was able to regurgitate that information when it was needed. But I wasn't experiencing real learning. Real learning would have involved action and application. Real learning would have meant that I could connect what was being learned to something that was meaningful to me or something that could be applied outside of the classroom in the real world.

> School should be a place where students go to pursue their passions, chase dreams, and create futures.

We have to find ways to move beyond what school has been and move toward all that it can be. For me, it was most often about compliance, but it can be about so much more than that. It can be about empowerment. You've heard this word several times throughout the book already, but I wanted to take a deep dive into what this should like in the classroom and what it means for today's learners. School should be a place where students go to pursue their passions, chase dreams, and create futures. Anything less than that implies that we don't value our students enough to create the change that this generation desperately needs right now.

Managing Versus Leading

I can remember a few of my teachers who did help me make connections to the real world through application. I remember the teachers who had conversations and gave me valuable information that made the learning relevant to me as a learner. Unfortunately, those teachers were few and far between. The status quo has been to give the information, assess to see who mastered the concept, and intervene when necessary. Rarely do we stop to think about the connections being made.

What if we changed the conversation? What if instead of simply expecting students to listen and then prove that they did so, we began asking them what and how they want to learn? What if we gave them the power to drive the learning and helped them invest in their own learning? I think that most of us would agree that students should want to participate in a learning experience because it's engaging—not because of the consequences that will happen if they don't.

There is a great quote that says, "Leaders become great, not because of their power, but because of their ability to empower others." As educators, we are the leaders of our learners. There is a big difference between managers and leaders (see Table 3). Managers are in charge; they tend to want to run things. Learners don't need to be managed if they are engaged. I think it's time that we stop talking about managing students and start talking about leading learners.

REFLECT

Are you a manager or leader? If you are a manager, what can you do to move more toward being a leader?

_____

_____

_____

_____

As leaders, we must find ways to empower our learners. In doing so, we will set them up to experience the real, meaningful learning that so many of our students want and deserve to experience during the school day.

Telling students what to learn is neat and tidy. We give; they take. Giving them a reason to learn is a different story. It's messy, as that reason might be different for every single learner. Students might be easily convinced that the learning is valuable, or they may see it is as a complete waste of their time. If the learning experience is designed well through personalization, there shouldn't need to be much con-

Table 3

Managers Versus Leaders

Managers	Leaders
Tell students what to learn	Give students a reason to want to learn
Focus on the details	See the big picture
Give approval/disapproval	Give feedback
Want to be in control	Work to inspire trust
Focus on goals	Inspire new growth

Note. Adapted from McKale, 2016.

vincing. Regardless of what the case may be, giving students a reason will make the learning authentic.

We often focus on details in the classroom. We move through the standards one at a time, ensuring that our students have mastered each one before moving on to another. We forget that, sometimes, the big picture is more valuable than the details. Outside of the classroom, our learners do not use the standards as separate details. They use all of their learning to solve problems, design solutions, and engage in experiences that require them to use every content area simultaneously.

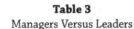

EMPOWER

How could meaningful learning be incorporated into your classroom? What would it look like to teach the big picture?

_____

_____

_____

_____

_____

Providing Feedback

Stamps . . . I can still remember the smell of the stamps that my teacher would use as she graded our papers. She had a green smiley face and a red sad face. We all knew what we were aiming for and what we had to do to get the green smiley face. Correct answers were the goal, and there wasn't much room for error. Oftentimes, the stamps were all that we received at the top of the paper, although they sometimes had a number grade as well. When I think about how I felt when I received a paper with either stamp reaction, there is not a lot of emotion attached. Sure, I was disappointed if I received a red sad face, but I remember not always knowing what I could have done differently or caring, for that matter.

Feedback provides a different experience. It's not about approval or disapproval but about growth. What feedback can be given to ensure that the learner understands what could have been done differently, or what questions does the learner need to ask to really understand this concept or idea? Feedback given quickly gives reason for action. It encourages students to do something, respond, or engage.

> Feedback . . . encourages students to do something, respond, or engage.

Grades without feedback are like doctors diagnosing someone but not writing a prescription. Can you imagine going to the doctor and hearing him say, "You have pneumonia. You need to work on that"? Of course not. We expect a doctor to give us ideas or suggestions for us to get better. Now, there are definitely times when the advice can be taken or ignored. A doctor may tell his patient that she needs to quit smoking. It's great advice, but the goal has to be completed by the patient, not the doctor.

There is definitely a place for this type of feedback in the classroom. It's important to know when to tell your learners to figure it out and when to offer feedback or a prescription to help them move in the right direction. This is different for every learner. Some need less feedback, and some need more. Knowing your students well provides you with the perspective you need to know when to offer feedback and when to sit back and let them struggle through the situation.

REFLECT

Do you give feedback or approval/disapproval? What can you do to move toward giving more feedback?

_____

_____

_____

_____

Goals and Growth

It's easy as an educator to want to be in control. As we talked about in the previous chapter, letting go of some of that control is what messy learning is all about. I don't believe that letting go of the control means that you don't have high expectations for your learners. However, it's about setting those high expectations and inspiring trust—in other words, helping students understand that you trust them enough to let them make some decisions and know themselves well enough as a learner to drive their own learning.

Focusing on goals is not a bad thing. However, if we get so focused on the goals that we ignore the growth, our learners will never appreciate the journey. Archery is a competitive sport and activity that many people find to be very fulfilling. The idea of hitting a target and reaching a goal can be very satisfying. However, very few people hit that target without lots of practice, work, and, ultimately, growth. They get closer and closer to the target until BAM! One day they hit it. If they hit their target the first time that they ever attempt archery, it's just luck. But when they hit the target after lots of work and time spent developing their skills, it's a big moment.

The same is true for learning. When it comes easily, it might not be as meaningful. However, when a learner is able to see his or her growth and appreciate the process, reaching that goal is big moment.

REFLECT

Would your learners say that your focus is on goals or growth? What would be their evidence?

_____

_____

_____

_____

Striving for Empowerment

Ultimately, leaders empower and managers dictate. Leaders will create change and managers are content with the status quo. As educators, the status quo should never be good enough. We should want more for our learners and encourage them to want more for themselves. In doing so, we will truly begin to lead them through empowerment. And when that happens, it's hard not to absolutely love going to work every day.

So, I know what you might be thinking after reading some of these things. It all sounds great and makes sense, but how do you empower a generation of learners who have been programmed to believe that school is all about compliance? These students have learned to play the game, and many of them can play it well.

Think about it this way. Imagine yourself visiting another country. Everything about the country is different . . . the language, the food, the culture, and even the transportation. You have two options. You can continue to dig your heels in and do things the way that you did in your home country. You can continue to speak your language, but no one will understand you. You can try to make the recipes you made at home, but you might not be able to find all of the ingredients. Finally, you can drive on the side of the road that is familiar, but it might cause an accident because everyone else is doing something different.

Or you can change the way that you do things. You can learn the new language so that you can communicate well, try new foods with new ingredients, and drive in a way that may be uncomfortable but keeps you alive. Changing the way that we do things opens the door for new ideas and new perspectives. If we don't begin to make empowerment a priority in our classrooms,

> Changing the way that we do things opens the door for new ideas and new perspectives.

we are preparing our students to experience that feeling of being in a new country when they go beyond the school experience. They will be so familiar with compliance that they will not know what to do or how to respond when they are required to take ownership of their own learning.

Do you remember cassette tapes? It wasn't long ago that we were moving to a new house, and my boys lifted up a box and my Bon Jovi cassette tapes fell out. One of them picked up the tapes and said, "What in the world is this?" I explained what a cassette tape was and that we actually had to wait for the radio DJ to play our favorite songs. Then, we would press play and record at the same time, hoping we would be able to get the entire song. They just looked at me like I had lost my mind.

What would your students say if you walked into class and handed them a cassette tape? First, they would say "What is this?" Then, they might say, "I can't use this. I don't have a cassette player." And guess what, they would be right (see Figure 2). Isn't this exactly what we are doing in the classroom if we continue to ask today's learners to learn in the same way that past generations did? We are giving them information that they can Google. We are asking them to use strategies that they will never use again outside of the classroom. What will they be able to do with that information outside of the classroom, and who is going to answer to them when they realize that they can't use what they have learned?

When we make empowerment the priority in our classrooms, we ask our students to change the way they see school. It might feel foreign, even uncomfortable, at first. It will not be easy to move from being spoon-fed information, strategies, and assignments to self-reflecting, self-assessing, and, ultimately, real learning. It will feel as though they have been dropped into a foreign country and will feel very different. But just as one becomes acclimated to a different culture, our students will become acclimated to this new way of learning. Instead of asking for answers, they will begin to ask for resources. Instead of regurgitating information, they will begin asking the "why" behind the information. They will begin to take the lead in their own learning, and when that happens, we should be not only excited but also confident that we have created empowered learners.

Teaching the same way that we did 20 years ago is like handing kids a cassette tape and expecting them to have a way to play it.

Figure 2. Teaching today's learners.

The 3 E's

Designing Meaningful
Learning Experiences

WHAT does it look like to design a meaningful learning experience? Many teachers are so familiar with writing lesson plans in a specific way that we focus more on what we are teaching rather than the "why" and the "how" behind what we are teaching. As we've addressed, Gen Zs need to understand the "why" behind what they are learning. In doing so, they are able to connect with the learning to find meaning and relevance.

I absolutely love podcasts. I listen to them on the way to work, on the way home from work, any chance that I get. However, I don't choose just any podcast. I don't listen to something that isn't meaningful to me. Instead, I choose to listen to the podcasts that are engaging, are empowering, and give me the information that I need right now. I tune in when podcasters start talking about things that I am experiencing or that I know I will be experiencing soon. I tune out when they start talking about things that I can't use right now and may never use in my lifetime. And, sometimes if this is the case, I turn them completely off.

Our students react the same way. They aren't going to tune in to information that they can Google when they get home or watch a video about on YouTube when they actually need the information. They are going to tune in when we find ways to connect what is being learned to their lives right now. Connecting to their "right now" is how we make learning meaningful. In order to do this, we have to know our students well and understand who they are as a generation of learners. So many of us feel uncomfortable with this because we have no idea what our students feel connected to. They might be especially connected to extracurricular activities, such as sports or a specific club. Their connections might involve a love of animals or serving others. Maybe they love sharing their ideas and creations on social media. Regardless of what that connection is, it's okay not to know what your students are connected to; it's not okay to not find out. Talk to them, watch them, get to know them as a generation, and be willing to be open-minded as you find ways to connect the learning to their everyday lives.

It's okay not to know what your students are connected to; it's not okay to not find out.

I believe that many of today's learners are willing to share what will work for them as learners and what will not. For example, the teen think tank WeRGenZ was created to give insight into what is meaningful to Gen Zs. You can find out more about WeRGenZ on Twitter or Instagram @WeRGenZ, as well as online at https://wergenz.com. Many of today's learners, however, have played the school game for so long that they don't even know what their options are. They've never taken the time to consider themselves as a learner. They simply see themselves as a student going through the motions. They've never considered what would work best or provide them with the most meaningful learning experience in the classroom. Instead, they simply comply with what is being done day in and day out, or maybe they don't. But if you give your students the opportunity and push them outside of their comfort zones just a bit so that they are able to see themselves as individual learners, I believe that they will be willing to share what they know about themselves so that they can experience the learning that they know that they need.

In order to share this information, learners must be self-aware. They need to be given time and experiences that will result in self-awareness and an understanding of who they are as a learner. Thrively (http://www.thrively.com) is a wonderful online tool that identifies student strengths, as well as their interests and what they aspire to become. It features great information for students, teachers, and parents. The DIRT Survey (https://www.iidc.indiana.edu/cedir/dirt/index.php) is a great way to encourage middle school and high school learners to identify themselves as Doers, Influencers, Relaters, or Thinkers. In doing so, they are also able to explore how to relate to and collaborate with others who are different than themselves. This survey is great for educators to take as well. Knowing who you are helps brings clarity to so many situations and conversations.

But how do you actually begin designing meaningful learning experiences for your students? Consider the 3 E's—engage, experience, and empower. They are easy to remember, and each one of them gives today's learners a reason and a way to make connections.

- **Engage:** How can my students be engaged in ways that will make them want to learn?
- **Experience:** What experience can be designed to give my learners a reason to want to invest in the learning?
- **Empower:** How can my learners be empowered to use what they learned outside of the classroom?

Which one of the 3 E's do you feel would be most powerful in your classroom? Why?

_____

_____

_____

_____

Engage

Engaging today's learners is by no means an easy task. If they are not engaged immediately, it is easy for them to check out and become distracted or even a behavior problem. Knowing that they have an attention span of only 8 seconds (BCM Partnership, 2015) is even more reason for us to find ways to grab their attention as soon as they walk through the door. I think back on my own classroom, and I can remember spending the first few minutes of class preparing myself. I would be getting things set up, taking attendance, and saying things like, "I'll start class as soon as you guys decide to be quiet." It's funny to think that I really thought that my students were so anxious to start class that they were going to get quiet. Of course they weren't. If they could postpone learning by being loud and disruptive, they were going to do just that. The reality, however, is that they were not excited about what we were going to do each day because I had not given them any reason to be.

Later in my career, I began to realize that if I would get students' attention as soon as they walked in the door, I was much more likely to hold that attention throughout the class period. Instead of waiting for them, I did the best that I could to engage them as soon as class began. What could I say that would make them want to be in class? How could I build anticipation and excitement before class even got started?

Dave Burgess, the author of *Teach Like a Pirate* (2012), created several hooks for educators to use to engage their learners. The following are just a few examples of the many that are shared throughout the book:

1. The Safari Hook involves taking your class outside and learning beyond the walls of the classroom.
2. The Mozart Hook involves using music to engage learners.
3. The Student Hobby Hook involves using student interests to help them make connections to what is being learned.

Using these hooks helps educators understand how to engage their students from the moment they walk in the door. It might feel a little bit awkward at first doing something that you've never done before, and it may even be a little weird for your learners. They will wonder what you are doing and why you are doing it. But once you have their attention and can connect whatever it is you are doing to what is going to be learned that day, they will be on the edge of their seats waiting to see what comes next.

In a blended learning environment, a hook can even be shared before students walk in the door. Send a video the day before with a teaser about what they can expect and look forward to the next day. The Literacy Shed (https://www.literacyshed.com), TED-Ed (https://ed.ted.com), and BrainPOP (https://www.brainpop.com) are all great places to find videos that can be shared before or during a learning experience. Ask students to bring something to class with them that will have them wondering what in the world they will possibly be doing to use that item. For example, if you are studying three-dimensional shapes, you might ask students to bring pictures of where they have been before on vacation or somewhere that they would like to go. As part of the learning experience, ask them to find all of the geometric figures in the photo. If you are introducing expository writing, bring in peanut butter and jelly. Have the ingredients and utensils on each students desk as they come into class. Ask students to actually make the sandwich as they write the process for doing so. Best part of this assignment? Allowing them to eat the sandwiches in class, of course! After using these hooks and understanding how they work, you will be creating your own hooks in no time.

REFLECT

What is something that you can do in your classroom immediately to hook your students in the first 8 seconds of class? How will you give them a reason to want to be there?

_____

_____

_____

_____

Experience

What if your classroom was such an experience that your students took selfies outside the classroom door before going in to share on social media? Think about it . . . this happens all of the time with the things today's learners are excited about. They take a picture before going into amusement parks, they take a picture before going to sporting events, and, in Texas, we even take selfies with a beaver at a gas station.

Let me explain. In Texas, we have these huge gas stations called Buc-ee's. One night, my sweet friend Cory Camp sent me a message asking if I had ever noticed that Buc-ee's does not post its gas prices by the road. After some conversation, we realized that Buc-ee's doesn't have to post its prices or try to convince people to stop because it has created an experience. Almost everyone in Texas knows that if you are traveling and need to stop for gas, Buc-ee's is where you want to be. You see, Buc-ee's has taken a mundane activity (getting gas) and made it an experience by giving its customers reasons to want to be there. Each Buc-ee's convenience store has amazing restrooms, wonderful on-the-road snacks, and even t-shirts adorned with the Buc-ee's mascot, Buc-ee the Beaver.

Activity and *experience*, the words themselves are very different. An activity is defined as something that a person or group does. An experience is an event or occurrence that leaves an impression. Isn't that just what we want to do? Don't we want to leave an impression on our learners? In doing so, we will create experiences that they will remember because of the connection that was made. I believe that if we can just shift our mindsets from writing lesson plans and creating activities to designing experiences, things will begin to change. I remember when I first learned about creating experiences from Dave Burgess and it made complete sense. Doesn't designing an experience sound so much more fun than writing a lesson plan, anyway?

Creating an experience is not as difficult as it might seem. Sometimes, it's just a matter of taking things to the next level. Examples might include:

- looking at a picture of a tornado versus watching a 360°-video of a tornado on YouTube,
- seeing the Egyptian pyramids in a textbook versus visiting the pyramids virtually with 360Cities (https://www.360 cities.net),
- learning about angles on a worksheet versus learning about angles by coding a video game during Hour of Code using Code.org (https://code.org),
- understanding area and perimeter by reading word problems versus understanding area and perimeter by connecting virtually with an architect, and/or
- writing a story to be shared with the teacher versus writing a story to be shared with an authentic audience.

In short, an experience involves learning by doing. Passive learning is not meaningful and simply will not work for this generation of learners. Active learning that requires them to do something, act on something, or design and create something takes the learning to the next level and makes it real. When the learning is an experience, we have created a reason for students to invest.

REFLECT

Think about your own classroom. If you had to draw a pie graph to represent active learning and passive learning, what would it look like? Which would take up the largest part of the graph?

_____

_____

_____

_____

_____

_____

_____

Experiences are messy. They rarely go exactly as planned and often end up looking very different than what we had imagined. If the learning is truly student-driven, educators shouldn't be planning the experience from start to finish. Instead, we should share what needs to be learned and options for doing so, and then facilitate, ask questions, and guide our learners as they experience the learning in a way that is most meaningful for them. I believe that when we begin to see school as an experience instead of a place, real change will come.

EMPOWER ⚡

Think of a lesson or activity that you have planned for the near future. How can you take it to the next level and make it an experience?

_____

_____

_____

_____

Empower

The last part of designing a meaningful learning experience is finding ways to empower. As we talked about earlier in this book, empowerment is a big piece of the learning process. It's so important for our learners to feel confident in using what they have learned. We have to find ways to connect what was learned to life outside of the classroom and outside of school. In order to do this, we must know learners well. If we know what they experience outside of school, we are able to help them make those connections. What does empowerment look like?

- Challenge students to use #booksnaps (http://www.taram martin.com/booksnaps-snapping-for-learning), created by Tara Martin, to share what they are reading on social media. BookSnaps give students an opportunity to use Bitmojis, GIFs, emojis, and more to share reflections on what they are reading on social media.
- Ask students to find real examples of math vocabulary, take pictures, and post them on a virtual bulletin board.

- Give students opportunities to use what they've learned to solve real-world problems. Check out https://www.global goals.org to find ways to help students make connections to those problems and consider what they can do to create change.
- Create a place within your LMS (learning management system), like Google Classroom or Canvas, for students to showcase the connections that they make when they are not in the classroom.
- Allow students to share learning and connections by writing a blog that is shared with the world. In doing so, they will have the opportunity to write both inside and outside of the classroom for an authentic audience.

We can also empower our learners by giving them more ownership of their own learning. This can be done by having student-led conferences. Student-led conferences give students the opportunity to take the lead and share what they are learning and what they need to improve (Edutopia, 2015). Instead of a group of adults sitting around talking about a student who isn't there, a student-led conference involves the student in every possible way.

During a student-led conference, students might share how they feel about school, what they have learned, what their goals are, and what they plan to do to reach those goals. They might share a digital portfolio or work that represents their learning well. In asking students to share these things, we help them understand that, although teachers are there to assist and guide them, ultimately, only they have to the power to do what needs to be done. Only they can meet the goals that they have set and experience learning that will be most beneficial to them in the future.

Designing Meaningful Learning Experiences With the 3 E's

The three E's give educators a framework for creating experiences that will engage today's learners by empowering them to use what they have learned. Unfortunately, while we are sitting around talking about change, our students are sitting in the classroom begging for a different experience. They are asking for experiences that will prepare them not only for a test but also for their futures. They are willing to learn, but they will not comply to a system that does not work for them.

So, let's stop just talking about change and start doing something about it. Making learning meaningful is—and should be—about so much more than knowing the latest buzzwords and technology tools. Observation and conversation will help you know students well so that you can design experiences that will make an impact. It really is as simple as knowing them well and designing experiences that will result in meaningful learning. Let's design experiences that students will talk about for days, create opportunities for them to make connections that they never imagined that they would make in the classroom, and give them a reason to want to be at school every day. In doing so, we will finally begin to the see the change that is so desperately needed.

> Let's design experiences that students will talk about for days.

The 4 C's + 1 R

Collaboration, Communication, Creativity, Critical Thinking, and Reflection

SO many skills that past generations were expected to naturally have are disappearing because of the culture and society that today's learners live in. I don't believe that Gen Z students are without all of these skills. The skills just look very different than they did for many learners of the past. Gen Z learners collaborate virtually, communicate via text messages, create digital products, think critically about the world around them, and need to reflect rather than simply remember in order for something to be meaningful.

These skills are the 4 C's—collaboration, communication, creativity, and critical thinking (National Education Association, 2010)—and 1 R—reflection (see Figure 3). But how do we address these skills in our classrooms? What can we do to make these a priority while still addressing the standards and concepts that must be taught? It's just a matter of weaving these into our learners' daily experiences. It is imperative that these skills are practiced and utilized every single day.

It's a good idea to have the 4 C's + 1 R posted wherever you design learning experiences. Write them on a sticky note, an index card, or whatever is most convenient and easy for you to access. If they are always right in front of you, it will be easy remember to weave them into whatever you are planning each and every day for your learners. Although it's not necessary to use all of the 4 C's + 1 R in every single experience, it's important to weave in as many as you can.

ENGAGE

Where can you post the 4 C's + 1 R so that you will remember to weave them into the learning experiences that you design for your students?

_____

_____

Collaboration

Collaborating is not something that all students do well. Many gifted students, for example, do not like to collaborate with other students either because they are expected to have all of the right answers or because they feel like they have the right answers and no one will listen to them. Collaboration and groupwork are different. Groupwork involves a teacher putting students into groups to complete an assignment. Collaboration is the coming together of a group of learners to solve a problem that may or may not have a correct answer. I believe that there is a place for both in the classroom. However, without practicing collaboration, our learners enter the real world thinking that they do not need others to help them solve problems. They become limited in what they can do because they are

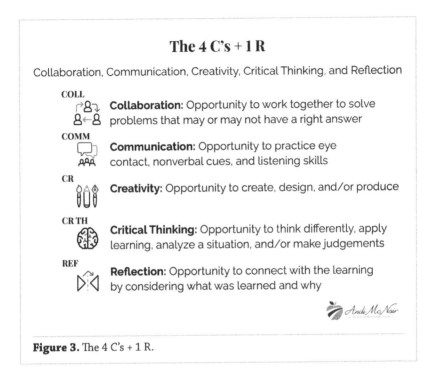

Figure 3. The 4 C's + 1 R.

not familiar with the idea of using others' strengths to solve specific problems.

Encouraging collaboration is as simple as giving your learners opportunities to solve real problems. Working together will strengthen classroom culture and help students understand their own weaknesses. I have definitely worked with people who do not know how to collaborate and aren't aware of how to use others' strengths to make up for their own weaknesses. These are the people who are hard to be around because they seem to think that they know everything about everything. They are the people whom you hope do not get put in your group on a team project.

> Working together will strengthen classroom culture and help students understand their own weaknesses.

Work is becoming more collaborative. Many businesses understand that employees work better together. Cubicles are being replaced by collaborative spaces, coworking spaces are popping up everywhere, and collaboration is becoming an expectation instead of just a good idea. One example of this is Apple's employee performance reviews. Apple evaluates its employees based on three categories: teamwork, innovation, and results (Sneckner, 2015). If an employee struggles with teamwork, that will most definitely be reflected on his or her evaluation and ultimately determine the likelihood of receiving a raise or even keeping his or her job.

REFLECT

Do you believe that there is a difference between group work and true collaboration? If so, how can you help your learners understand the difference?

_____

_____

_____

_____

Communication

Communicating with others seems like something that we are all able to do. However, we have a generation of learners who spend the majority of their time talking to each other on the other side of a screen. Their ability to communicate well face-to-face has been impaired by the fact that they do not have to do it very often. Because of this, it is extremely important that we give them opportunities to practice real communication in the classroom every single day.

Talk to your learners and model eye contact and listening skills so that they begin to see what they should be doing when they are communicating. Allow them to talk to outside experts, their peers, and anyone else who might give them an opportunity to practice communicating and communicating well. Finally, encourage them to communicate well with each other by giving them time to do so. If they are constantly being told to be quiet in class, how will they ever improve their communication skills? Messy learning isn't quiet. It's sometimes loud and chaotic, and that's okay.

> Messy learning isn't quiet. It's sometimes loud and chaotic, and that's okay.

EMPOWER ⚡

What can you do immediately in your classroom to encourage students to intentionally practice communication?

_____

_____

_____

_____

Creativity

I think that sometimes we assume that this generation of learners is not creative. We make assumptions like this because they do not produce art the same way that we did. Just the opposite is true. Today's learners are very creative. They simply create differently than older generations did or, maybe, still do. They create by designing video games, filming and editing videos for YouTube, writing storylines for digital comic books, and so much more. The potential is there for them to do so much more with their creations than past learners were ever able to do. Like we talked about in Chapter 3, this generation has the ability to instantly share their creativity with the world.

So, what does creativity look like in today's classroom? It's about giving students options, offering choices for how they show their learning. Why do we feel the need to dictate how a learner shares that he or she has learned what has been taught? Let's let students make that decision. The truth is that not all learners like to create, but many of them do. Some of them are passionate about music, others absolutely love creating art, and many of them have creative skills that we never see because there is never a time in the classroom for them to showcase those skills.

Offer your learners a menu of options for sharing their learning, and make one of the squares a free choice so that they can come up with their own ideas (see Figure 4). I think you will be surprised by how willing they are to engage in a learning experience when they feel like they have some ownership. As long as they can show in some way that they understand what is being learned, why do we care how that is done? Asking students to show their learning in a way that they cannot connect with is like asking someone who doesn't like music to write a song. Not only will they be completely lost, but also they will be frustrated throughout the entire process, resulting in negative feelings toward the learning.

EMPOWER

Create your own menu of options for your students choose from in order to show mastery. What can you ask them to create in order to show what they know?

Menu of Learning Options

Code a video game using Scratch to show what you learned	Write a song to show what you know	Create a piece of art that demonstrates understanding
Write a book on Book Creator to explain today's topics to your classmates	**Free Choice**	Create a website on Weebly to share your learning with the world
Share a video on Flipgrid with a reflection of your learning today	Bring something from outside of the classroom that represents our learning and be prepared to explain	Design, make, or produce a 3-D product to demonstrate your understanding

Menu of Learning Options For Nonreaders

Figure 4. Examples of menus.

Critical Thinking

Although creative thinking is very important, critical thinking is important as well. Critical thinking is something that we talk a lot about in education. I fear that we talk about it a lot but don't give our learners authentic opportunities to practice the skill as often as they need. The keyword is *authentic*. I tend to struggle with workbooks or worksheets that claim to engage students in the critical thinking skill without encouraging another step for learners to actually do something with learning through application. Let me explain why.

The Foundation for Critical Thinking (n.d.) defined critical thinking as "the intellectually disciplined process of actively and skillfully conceptualizing, applying, analyzing, synthesizing, and/or evaluating information gathered from, or generated by, observation, experience, reflection, reasoning, or communication, as a guide to belief and action." Some of my favorite words in this definition are *actively*, *apply*, *experience*, *reflection*, and *communication*. Those skills are difficult to apply on a worksheet. They are, however, very easily addressed through authentic experiences that set learners up to practice them.

Here's an example:

- **Teacher A** gives her students an assignment to take a stance on an issue that is somewhat controversial. She asks them to write about their stance and share why they feel the way that they do. After doing so, the students turn their papers into the teacher. She grades them and returns them. In her lesson plans, she checks off addressing critical thinking for the day or week and doesn't give it a second thought.

- **Teacher B** gives his students the same assignment. He asks them to blog about their stance and share their perspective with the world, without sharing their name or the name of their school anywhere in the post. He then plans for students with different perspectives to share their ideas with the class in a debate-style experience. In doing so, he asks those that are listening and watching to offer feedback. He also offers opportunities for the students sharing to reflect on what they did and what could have been done differently to convince others to see things from their perspective. Finally, he asks his students to find a way to do something with their perspective. If they feel as though animals should not be locked in cages at the zoo, they can write a letter to communicate with their local zoo and other decision makers to share their thoughts. They might even design what they think the zoo might look instead to conceptualize what it is that they think should happen.

Do you see the difference? Teacher A allowed her students to experience the surface-level version of critical thinking. Teacher B took his learners beyond the surface and allowed them to dive deep into not just thinking critically, but also engaging in an authentic experience that likely resulted in meaningful learning.

I know your first thought might be *time*. How would I ever have the time in the classroom to spend that much time on one experience? If done well, this type of experience will address many of the standards that would be addressed if the teacher were addressing a standard each day. Learners will be applying their standards, and the teacher will know what is being learned through observation and conversation. It's messy, it involves risk-taking, and it may be uncomfortable for everyone when first introduced. But, if this type of learning becomes the standard, so will critical thinking. It will become easier and easier to weave critical thinking into learning experiences throughout the school year.

REFLECT

Do you provide opportunities in your classroom for your learners to think critically? What do those opportunities look like?

_____

_____

_____

_____

Reflection

The one R in the 4 C's + 1 R represents *reflection*. Reflection is very important and something that I believe should happen every single day in the classroom. Teaching students to reflect is no easy task, but when they are able to reflect versus being able to remember, the learning becomes personal. Students understand on a much deeper level.

When students reflect, they make stronger connections to what is being learned. Without those connections, students have a harder time remembering what was learned at school after leaving class. Today's learners have access to so much information outside of the classroom. As soon as school is out, and often before, they are on their phones watching YouTube videos and looking at posts on Snapchat and Instagram. The reality is that when they get on their devices and watch 10–20 YouTube videos and look at hundreds of posts, there is only so much storage space in their brains. It only makes sense that when there is no more room, the first thing to be pushed out is something that was not meaningful to them or something that did not result in a connection.

So how do we help them make those connections? How do we encourage reflection and help our learners move past simply remembering in order to make the learning meaningful? I think the first step is to acknowledge that there is a difference between reflection and remembering. Remembering is what students did and how; however, reflection is what students learned and why. Next, it's just a matter of being super intentional about providing opportunities in the classroom for purposeful reflection. This means that as educators, we don't value content cramming so much that we teach bell to bell with no time for reflection. Instead, we value reflection enough to stop mid-sentence if necessary to allow time at the end of every class period for students to reflect and make connections to what was learned. This can be done by having students write about experiences on Kidblog, sharing a short video on Flipgrid, or simply turn-ing and talking to each other about a reflection question that is posted or given using the reflection question cards from Tony Vincent (see https://learninginhand. com/blog/2013/7/5/roll-reflect-with-qr-codes).

Putting It All Together

Designing experiences while considering the 4 C's + 1 R will prepare learners for not only their futures but their "right now." These skills are imperative as they create relationships, engage in extracurricular activities, and engage in experiences outside of the classroom. These skills should not be optional or seen as separate from the learning that happens every day in the classroom. Instead, find ways to seamlessly weave them into everything that is done each and every day so that they become a natural part of who our learners become.

Learning by Doing

Genius Hour and Meaningful Makerspaces

LEARNING by doing can be achieved in so many ways throughout the school day. However, there are two movements happening in education right now that are proving to be game changers in today's classrooms.

Both of these movements are built upon the foundation of innovation and opportunities to create during the school day. In my classroom, our definition of innovation was creating something new or making something better. Innovation is a building block for growth. When our students are given opportunities to innovate, they are giving opportunities to grow. I think many of us can think of students who are not given the opportunity to grow during the school day. They are sitting in classrooms listening to things

> Innovative learning experiences could simply be what learning looks like in today's classrooms.

that they already know. We are stifling their learning, and they certainly aren't given opportunities to innovate or develop solutions for real-world problems.

Unfortunately, we currently see opportunities to innovate and create as "extra" experiences. In other words, many times, we only get to this type of learning if we get through all of the traditional things that need to be done. This type of learning is also often reserved for learners who do not need intervention or need something "extra." This doesn't have to be the case. Innovative learning experiences could simply be what learning looks like in today's classrooms.

In many cases, when students who are unable or unwilling to learn through compliance-driven, traditional learning situations are able to learn by doing, they begin to flourish. As educators, the majority of us have had a noncompliant gifted learner who just won't play the game, and we've all had struggling learners who are unable to learn the way that we are teaching. We've become really good at placing labels on students in the education system. The reality is that sometimes they don't need a label, they need a different learning experience. The fact that they aren't immediately successful on a worksheet doesn't always mean that they don't or can't understand what is being learned. It may just mean that they need to be able to demonstrate the learning in a different way, and for many of our learners, that different way is application.

ENGAGE

Can you think of a learner in your classroom who doesn't play the school game well and would benefit from learning by doing? Spoiler alert: Don't be surprised if every single learner comes to mind!

_____

_____

Genius Hour

Genius Hour is passion-based learning. It involves giving students real opportunities to pursue their passions and learn while doing so. I have a personal connection with Genius Hour, as it was the most powerful strategy that I ever implemented in my classroom. When I gave my learners an opportunity to learn by creating solutions to things that bothered them, I saw learning become meaningful. I watched gifted students who were bored and disengaged come to life and find new ways to learn. I realized that many struggling students were able to learn concepts and skills by doing what they were never able to demonstrate on a worksheet. Compliant students were forced outside of their comfort zones and empowered to take ownership of their learning, and noncompliant learners were finally given an opportunity to learn on their own terms.

My students pursued their passions using a process that we called the six P's (see Figure 5). They found their passion, planned their pursuit, pitched their idea to the class, worked on a project to develop a product, and finally gave a presentation (McNair, 2017b).

If I'm completely honest, Genius Hour was my first full dive into messy learning—and it was definitely a mess! I was so uncomfortable and oftentimes wondered if what

> Genius Hour is passion-based learning.

I was doing even fell under the category of learning. But then I began to look deeper. I began to listen to conversations, ask questions, and collaborate with my students. And, as I did, I realized that they were learning more than ever before.

It didn't look like what I had known before. Students weren't listening to me talk and then proving that they had done so by regurgitating information. They weren't proving on a worksheet 25 times

---

Genius Hour 6 P's

1. **Passion:** What do you want to learn about? What do you think is interesting? What can you get excited about?

2. **Plan:** Who will be your outside expert? What materials will you need to complete the project? What will you need to do each day to reach your goals?

3. **Pitch:** How will you share your idea with the class? How will you get us on board?

4. **Project:** It's time to dive in! What do you need to do today to move forward with your project? What are you creating, making, or designing?

5. **Product:** What did you create? What can you show us to demonstrate your learning?

6. **Presentation:** How do you plan to share your learning? Can you share your idea or project with others? What tools will you use to make your presentation engaging for the audience?

Figure 5. The 6 P's of Genius Hour. From *Genius Hour: Passion Projects That Ignite Innovation and Student Inquiry* (p. 16), by A. McNair, 2017, Waco, TX: Prufrock Press. Copyright 2017 by Prufrock Press. Reprinted with permission.

---

that they had mastered a particular skill. Instead, they were engaging in meaningful learning by actively doing something.

Many of my students designed projects around things that bothered them and developed ideas that would inspire change. Some of them pursued their passions of helping others through some form of action. For example, two of my students learned to sew as they made pillowcases for children who were in the hospital. Another student organized and managed a 5K for our community to run, as she raised money for local animal shelters. As I watched my students dive into these projects, I realized that learning for the sake of learning is not meaningful for today's learners. Learning in order to do something, however, develops a sense of purpose within students, and they are willing to do things that they would never do before.

Purpose should play a big role in today's classrooms. When students are driven by purpose rather than compliance, they are willing—willing to take risks, willing to work hard, and willing to learn through pursuit of their passions. Purpose is the foundation that supports passion, and without it, passion cannot be sustained. I believe that purpose is the foundation for everything done in the classroom. It is very closely related to relevance and plays an important role in a student's desire to learn.

REFLECT

What role does purpose play in your classroom right now, and what role would you like for it to play?

_____

_____

_____

_____

_____

I recently learned about benefit mindset. Buchanan (2016) described it as "a purpose-driven mindset that is redefining success from being the best in the world to being the best for the world" (para. 3). Just imagine if students could learn the standards while learning to be the best for the world. Genius Hour gives them an opportunity to do both. Educators are able to weave the standards into student projects while encouraging their learners to create something that will impact their campus, district, community, city, state, country, or maybe even the world.

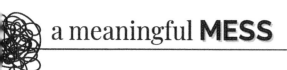

Makerspaces

Makerspaces are popping up in many districts and communities throughout the country. A Makerspace is defined as "a place where students can gather to create, invent, tinker, explore and discover using a variety of tools and materials" (Rendina, 2015, para. 5). Just like Genius Hour, a Makerspace involves messy learning and a willingness to let students find ways to develop their own solutions and find ways to "figure it out."

I recently saw a cartoon that showed a teacher saying, "I expect you all to be innovative, independent, and creative thinkers who do exactly as I say." This is a perfect representation of what many of our learners experience every day. We are talking the talk but not walking the walk. We tell students what they need to be but don't give them opportunities to be that in the classroom. We encourage innovation but continue to ask students to solve problems using the strategy that they were given. We ask them to be independent but continue to spoon-feed them information during the school day. Finally, we want them to be creative thinkers but rarely give them opportunities to think outside of the box or differently about real problems.

Meaningful Makerspaces give students real opportunities to make connections. Learners create, make, and design while working toward a solution that may or may not exist. In doing so, they learn to collaborate with students they may have never talked to before, create in ways that they never imagined, and take risks they would have never been willing to take in a traditional classroom.

Meaningful Makerspaces:
- engage learners in purposeful problem solving and design,
- give students an opportunity to learn by doing,
- have standards embedded into the experience,
- give students opportunities to connect and reflect, and
- focus on questions rather than answers.

Even if there is not a true Makerspace on your campus, you can create a space or cart in your classroom to be used by your learners. There are great resources out there and places to find ideas and experiences for your very own Makerspace. Wonderopolis has maker experiences embedded into its summer Camp Wonderopolis (https://camp.wonderopolis.org). It also shares lessons and nonfiction reading selections to partner with each activity so that learners are able to practice reading comprehension and vocabulary as part of the experience. Maker Camp (https://makercamp.com) shares many maker experiences, along with facilitation advice and reflection opportunities. Finally, DIY (https://diy.org) is all about making. Learners choose what they would like to explore and then choose from a variety of challenges that involve making and designing in order to do so.

Lacy Brejcha, a personal friend of mine, wrote a wonderful book about Makerspaces called *Makerspaces in School: A Month-by-Month Schoolwide Model for Building Meaningful Makerspaces* (2018). She shared her thoughts about Makerspaces and how they can be messy but also challenging and fun:

Makerspaces force students to leave their comfort zones and are challenging, fun, busy, messy, loud . . . basically controlled chaos! But don't let that deter you. . . . What stands out the most to me is that students are highly engaged and focused on what they are doing. Behavior is rarely a problem because students are so engaged. They question each other, question themselves, solve problems, and create. These are all high-level thinking skills that keep the brain engaged. Often times, an adult will come into my classroom and no students will even notice! They are so focused on and consumed with making and learning that outside stimuli go unnoticed. . . . Makerspaces are loud, fun, and messy—but controlled chaos. Expect that, and plan for it. (pp. 14, 131)

ENGAGE

Check out the hashtag #makered on Twitter. Find some ideas that you can incorporate in your own classroom and favorite those tweets so that you can revisit them later.

Focusing on the Process

Both the Genius Hour and Makerspace movements focus on the process rather than the product. Although both give students an opportunity to create or make a product, the end product is not necessary for learning to happen. I can think of many times that my students experienced failure or struggled and a product was not created. The reality, however, is that sometimes those students learned more than those who were able to coast through the process without any struggle at all. Chris Lehman says, "If you assign a project and get back 30 of the same thing, that's not a project, that's a recipe."

Too often in education, we have focused on the product because it is convenient. It has always made sense to give all students the same worksheet, grade them with the same key, and place a number grade at the top. This no longer makes sense. Student products should be different because students' process should be different depending on who they are as learners.

Focusing on the process of learning is more difficult. It requires us, as educators, to truly engage and collaborate with our learners. We must ask questions, give opportunities to reflect, and know them well as learners. It may be more difficult and require us to be more engaged to reach our learners, but it is so worth it. Never value the product more than the process. The process is how students learn to fail, reflect, and try again. In other words, it's how they learn how to learn. There is nothing more rewarding as an educator than to watch your students learn by changing the world or creating something that has never been created before.

> Never value the product more than the process.

Both Genius Hour and Meaningful Makerspaces are messy in every sense of the word. They are uncomfortable for both the educator and learner when first introduced. The power in the classroom shifts, and the learning begins to look, sound, and feel different. But if you look closely, listen well, and fully engage, you will begin to see that these opportunities to learn result in learning that may be messy, but more importantly, is very meaningful. I believe that this generation of learners has ideas that can change the world. It's just a matter of getting out of their way and giving them opportunities to learn by doing.

EMPOWER

Consider how you can implement Genius Hour, Makerspace, or both in your classroom to give your students opportunities to learn by doing.

_____

_____

_____

_____

Going Global

FOR years, students have learned from textbooks and work-sheets. They have read about faraway places and experiences with which they were not able to connect. As a student, I remember being very interested in Australia. I wanted to learn more, but all I had access to were images and stories. I remember one of my teachers encouraging me to send a letter requesting some travel brochures that would give me more information about Australia, and I was so excited. Anything beyond the traditional textbook information and encyclopedia pictures stirred something inside me that made me want to invest and go the extra mile to learn more.

Today's learners react the same way. Unlike myself as a student, they are very well aware of the digital information and experiences that they can access to learn so much more than they can from any textbook. We can't tell our students how a topic or concept is used in the real world and then distribute a worksheet. It doesn't make any sense for our students to sit in class solving fictional problems. Let's use the world as our textbook and break through the walls of the classroom so that learning has a purpose. As a result, our students will see value in what is being learned and will be able to carry that learning with them as they walk out of the classroom each and every day.

So, what does that look like? Just like everything else that I've suggested in this book, it's messy but very much worth it. Teaching from a textbook is nice and neat, and let's be honest, easy. I think about my son's baseball games and what is said when the players make a very routine play. Someone always says something like, "That was a textbook double play," or "That was a textbook bunt." What they mean is they executed the play exactly as expected and achieved the expected result. The play wasn't risky, and it wasn't difficult—just textbook. Let me put it this way. If you are preparing for a substitute teacher and all you have to write down in your lesson plans is the pages in the textbook that are to be read and the pages in the workbook that are to be completed, you are missing out on some huge opportunities to help your learners make connections to what is being learned.

> Let's use the world as our textbook and break through the walls of the classroom so that learning has a purpose.

Many educators, however, just aren't aware that these opportunities to help learners make meaningful connections exist. It's difficult to keep up with how quickly society and education itself are changing and hard to keep your head above water with so many expectations, standards, and concepts that have to be taught. But what if these could be taught while giving learners an opportunity to make meaningful connections? What if we could use our instant access to the world to give our learners opportunities to connect the dots? What if our students could learn about the world from the world?

In this chapter, I am going to share some very practical ways that the world can be brought into the classroom. The Global Goals for

Sustainable Development, virtual reality, outside experts, and classroom collaborations are powerful ways to break down the walls.

Global Goals

The 17 Global Goals for Sustainable Development (United Nations, 2015) were agreed upon by world leaders. The goals offer a framework to help your students understand what needs to change in our world and how they might have the ideas to impact that change. Some examples of the goals are no poverty, clean water and sanitation, sustainable cities and communities, and affordable and clean energy.

Introducing these goals to your learners and giving them an opportunity to discuss which of the goals are most important to them is a great place to start. Ask them why they think the goals are important or if they even think they are important. Then, allow them to justify their responses.

One possible way to integrate these into your classroom is to ask your students to choose one of these goals at the beginning of the year. As they learn throughout the year, ask them to connect what is being learned to the goal that they have chosen (e.g., "How can what you have just learned be used to impact the global goal that you have chosen?"). Allowing students to decide how the learning fits into something that they care about gives them a reason to want to invest. If they can connect what is being learned to the global goal that they have chosen, they will find value.

The World's Largest Lesson (http://worldslargestlesson.global goals.org) is a website that incorporates the Global Goals into experiences that can be used in the classroom to call our students to action. By clicking on Resource Library and choosing an age range, you are able to see sample lesson plans and ideas for incorporating the Global Goals into the classroom. One of my favorite experiences on the website is Design for Change: One Idea, One Week (http://cdn.worldslargestlesson.globalgoals.org/2016/06/Design-for-Change-One-Idea-One-Week.pdf).

This experience encourages empathy and innovation as it encourages learners to feel, imagine, do, and share. Over the course of 7 days, students experience each of these pieces as they find ways to make the world a better place. You might be thinking that this is starting to sound a lot like Genius Hour, which we discussed in the previous chapter, and you are right! This is a great place to start with Genius Hour, but it can also be used a standalone activity through which you can weave in different standards and skills that are currently be addressed in the classroom.

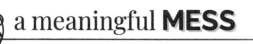

ENGAGE

Do you believe that your learners can create change? How could something like the World's Largest Lesson or the Global Goals impact their learning of the standards?

_____

_____

_____

_____

_____

_____

_____

_____

_____

_____

Virtual Reality

Virtual reality is another way to bring the world into the classroom, and it is very easy to do. I think we often assume that virtual reality is expensive or that we need specific devices and tools to make it happen in our own classrooms. However, some types of virtual reality can be experienced on every device, and students absolutely love it.

Let's think about my fixation on Australia when I was a student. Although the pictures that I received from the travel brochures were awesome at the time, how much cooler would it have been for me to experience the Great Barrier Reef using virtual reality? What if I could have used a device to feel like I was actually standing near Ayers Rock or the Sydney Opera House? The truth is, I would have been willing and able to learn whatever my teacher wanted me to learn if he or she could have connected it to that experience.

Today's learners love virtual reality, and it doesn't have to be fancy. Virtual reality experiences can be found on YouTube, Nearpod (https://nearpod.com), and many other platforms. One of my favorite VR resources is 360Cities (https://www.360cities.net). Using this website, students and educators are able to virtually experience places all over the world. Using the search feature allows users to look for specific landmarks, cities, and places. With the click of a button, they are transported into a 360°-experience within which they can look around and truly experience what it might be like to visit that specific location.

To learn more about virtual reality, you must connect with Jaime Donally. She is a personal friend of mine and my go-to person for all things AR/VR. Donally wrote *Learning Transported: Augmented, Virtual and Mixed Reality for All Classrooms* (2018). She shared that by using AR/VR "you can eliminate the limitations of locations or funding and take your students on virtual field trips to places like the Great Barrier Reef." You can take students anywhere that you want at any time using virtual reality. If that's not an experience, I don't know what is!

ENGAGE

Stop reading and visit https://www.360cities.net. Explore a place that you have always wanted to go to. How is this different than simply looking at a photograph?

_____

_____

_____

_____

_____

_____

_____

_____

_____

_____

Outside Experts

I think that outside experts are one of the most powerful ways that we can help our learners make connections. An outside expert might be an astronaut who shares how he or she used math in space, a dolphin trainer who talks about how he or she uses the scientific method to learn more about the creature, or a volcanology student who shares personal experiences about visiting volcanoes and what it's like to be up close and personal with them.

ENGAGE

Visit https://nepris.com/video/model-volcano-45888 and watch my students talk with an outside expert. Register for free so that you can access the video library. After watching for a few minutes, skip to the 21:49 mark, and watch as the expert shares a video of herself at a volcano. How do you think this type of experience might impact your learners?

_____

_____

_____

_____

Outside experts offer a perspective that we, as teachers, are unable to bring into the classroom unassisted. Teachers have not been trained to know everything about everything. Although we can't always give our students the information that they need to explore further or learn more, we can create and facilitate experiences that will help them do so.

Finding outside experts seems like a lot of work, and it can be if you aren't aware of the resources that are available to help you. Obviously, the best place to start is in your own community. Know your students and their families well enough to be able to make connections between what is being learned in the classroom to what they do every day outside of school. Maybe your students have family members who use what is being taught in the classroom in their everyday jobs. Inviting them in to share why it is important to learn what is being addressed in the classroom can change the way your learners experience the specific content or standard that is being learned.

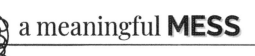
Tools like Nepris (https://www.nepris.com) make it easy to find outside experts. You simply log in, share what you are looking for, choose three times that will work for you and your students, and the site does the rest. Nepris even gives you an opportunity to choose the standards that you would like to see addressed throughout the experience. Ultimately, Nepris connects you and your students with an outside expert who uses Zoom to connect virtually and collaborate. I'm a huge fan of this platform, as it makes the outside expert experience realistic and easy for educators without it seeming like one more thing.

 My class also created a "Help Wanted" wall on Padlet (https://padlet.com/mcnairandi/experts) for finding outside experts. Padlet is a digital bulletin board that is very easy to use. Note that you are limited on the number of Padlets that you can create for free. We simply created the Padlet, posted what we were looking for in the experts, and shared the Padlet via social media. We also shared the Padlet with our local college and asked students to serve as our outside experts as well. This strategy worked really well, as I just asked the experts to fill out a Google Form if they were interested in collaborating with our class. We used form notifications to ensure that we were notified each time the form was filled out. I would then connect with the expert, set up a time for students to connect, and then moderate the experience.

Outside experts change the way that our learners see learning. It helps them see the "why" behind what is being taught. Is it messy? Sure . . . it's a little bit of extra work to find an expert. The expert may be long-winded or not what the students had in mind. However, hearing someone other than their teacher share why they need to know about what is being learned changes the experience and gives students a reason to buy in.

EMPOWER ⚡

What is a topic or concept that you have coming up in your own classroom that would be more meaningful if an outside expert was involved? How can you make that happen?

_____

_____

_____

_____

_____

_____

_____

_____

_____

_____

Classroom Collaborations

As we talked about in Chapter 2, Gen Z is a collaborative generation. These learners are connected on social media and realize the power of sharing and learning with others. Because of the technology that we have access to, we are no longer confined to only collaborating with other classrooms within our building. We can collaborate with classrooms from all over the world.

REFLECT

What technology do you currently have access to in your own classroom that you could use for collaboration with other classrooms (Chromebooks, iPads, webcams, desktops)?

_____

_____

_____

_____

Finding another classroom that is learning about something similar and connecting with those students is another way to expose students to different perspectives. Learning about something from a different perspective helps learners feel connected and part of a bigger picture than what they traditionally feel when they are isolated in their own classrooms surrounded by the same people day in and day out.

Connecting with other classrooms also exposes students to different cultures and parts of the world that they might not even know exist. Experiences like a Mystery Skype or Mystery Hangout can change the way that our students see the world. A Mystery Skype involves connecting with another classroom somewhere else in the world. Each classroom asks yes/no questions that will help students find out where the other classroom is located. I absolutely love Mystery Skypes because everyone gets to play. It involves all of the 4 C's + 1 R—collaboration, communication, critical thinking, and creativity—and, of course, it's important for students to reflect after the experience as well.

During a Mystery Skype, every student has a role. There are many opportunities for students to be involved as questioners, answerers, mappers, and more (Connell, 2014). One of the major benefits of a Mystery Skype is that learners are addressing so many different skills and learning more about geography through experience. Unfortunately, geography is not always a priority in many classrooms, but knowing where cities, states, countries, landmarks, and landforms are in the world is something that every learner should not only experience but also be expected to know fairly well.

Mystery Skype is loud, chaotic, and a little messy. However, I have seen some of my most disengaged learners become involved in ways that I never imagined. When students reflect on these experiences, it's often very surprising when they share what they have learned. I can remember reading students' reflections and being in awe of the connections that they made that I hadn't even thought of. In Figure 6, which is adapted from a response written by a student I worked with, you will see the student enjoyed the experience so much that "Very Good" just wasn't good enough. The student created her very own "Awesome" emoji. I think that when students begin making connections that you hadn't even planned, you begin to realize that this type of learning is worth every bit of planning and thinking outside of the box.

ENGAGE

Watch this YouTube video about Mystery Skype: https://youtu.be/eRf7_nX74PA. How do you think your learners might react to a learning experience similar to this one? Did Mr. Bedley share anything that reminds you of yourself as an educator?

_____

_____

_____

_____

_____

Figure 6. Example mystery Skype reflection. Adapted from Battistella (as cited in McNair, 2015).

There are many other ways that classrooms can collaborate across the globe. Check out Skype in the Classroom (https://education. microsoft.com/skype-in-the-classroom/overview) and choose Skype Collaborations. The collaborations are sorted by subject area, and you simply click on one that seems appropriate to learn more about. You can also create your own collaborations to share with other users. Using these tools gives educators peace of mind and aids in planning something that might otherwise seem quite daunting.

Another way that you can connect your classroom is by using a program called Empatico (https://empatico.org). Empatico is cen-tered around curiosity, empathy, and kindness. Using this program will encourage respectful communication and even critical thinking. Empatico connects learners through live video to create meaningful connections. What a great way to give students an opportunity to learn something new and work on skills like communication, collaboration, and reflection. I love that reflection is built into each activity through Empatico. This program is a great way to introduce learners to connecting online and creating experiences that your learners will remember for a very long time.

ENGAGE

Visit Empatico (https://empatico.org) and peruse the activities. Find one that you think might be meaningful for your learners. How will you use the activity in your classroom?

_____

_____

_____

_____

_____

_____

_____

Global connections are no longer just an option for today's learners. They must know to collaborate and learn with others outside of an organization (Adams, 2014). Because of the technology that we have access to in today's classrooms, we are able to bring the world into the classroom. In choosing not to do so, we are closing the door on opportunities that could truly engage and empower our students.

Reflection Versus Remembering

I visit a lot of classrooms. One of the words that I hear very often is *remember*. We ask questions like, "Do you remember when we talked about . . . ?" "Can you remember how to . . . ?" Merriam-Webster defined *remember* as "to bring to mind or think of again." I don't know about you, but I needed my students to do much more than just think of something again. I needed whatever they were doing or saying to actually reflect their learning. I needed it to make the learning apparent. In asking them to reflect, I was asking them to think more deeply by connecting with what was learned.

Most learners do not know to reflect naturally. They know to remember, regurgitate, recreate. In fact, they know how to reciprocate in the classroom, as they see it as a give and take: "The teacher gives me information, and I take it in. I give that information back to my teacher, and she takes a grade." That's how we have played the game for a very long time, and, in doing so, we have created learners who can regurgitate information but oftentimes can't apply what was learned. In other words, if something doesn't look exactly like it did on the worksheet that they practiced, they don't know what to do or how to do it.

Even our gifted learners like being asked to remember. If all they have to do is recall, chances are they are going to get the right answer. There's no risk, no opportunity to figure anything out, and no need to think critically about what is being learned. However, if we ask students to reflect and make a connection to the learning, we are pushing them beyond the status quo and toward becoming independent learners who value making connections.

Teaching Reflection

So how do you teach reflection? How do we encourage our learners to move beyond just remembering and dive deeper so that they can experience learning in a way that will be most meaningful? You can model reflection for your students and provide feedback on their reflections.

Model Reflection

Find ways to reflect on your own experiences, successes, and failures. John Dewey said, "We don't learn from an experience, we learn from reflecting on an experience." I love that quote because it makes so much sense. As we discussed earlier, if we choose to teach bell to bell and do not give any opportunity for reflection at the end of the class, we might as well ask our students to wad up whatever learning happened and throw it in the trash. Reflection is like waiting for paint to dry before touching it. If we touch it before it's dry, it's going to come off, and it's going to be messier than it needs to be. Learning is the same way. If we don't give it time to set or time to "dry," it falls right off.

Think about cooking steak. If we don't marinate the steak in a delicious marinade before we cook it, there is no flavor. If we simply rub the marinade on and don't give it time to set in, it will not change the flavor of the meat. It will just be plain and dry. We definitely don't want the learning that our learners experience in our classrooms to be plain and dry . . . yuck! We want it to be flavorful. We want them to reflect on what has been learned so that it sinks in. And if we are honest, if that doesn't happen, we have wasted our time and that of our students.

I remember the first time that I shared my blog with my students. One of my students said, "You actually write for fun?" I laughed and explained that I didn't necessarily enjoy writing (I still don't), but I do value reflection enough to share my story. My students spent some time looking through the blog and then asked why I wrote about things that didn't go well. We had a great discussion about how reflection is most powerful when you are reflecting on failure.

> Reflection is most powerful when you are reflecting on failure.

Provide Feedback

Reflection can also be taught by giving feedback on students' reflections. When I first began asking my students to reflect, they did so by blogging. As I read their blogs it was very clear that they were simply remembering what we did each day. They said things like, "Today I . . ." and then went on to tell me what they did. After I realized what was happening, we had a class meeting. I explained to my students that I was actually in class all day and saw what they had done. I laughed and pointed out that I had actually planned the experience, so I didn't just need them to recall what we had done. Instead, I needed to them to reflect on the connections that they made throughout the learning experience: "What did it mean to you? What will you do with what you have learned? What were some of your struggles?" Slowly but surely, they began to understand what reflection should look like and why it was so different than remembering.

Making Reflection a Priority

Make reflection the priority each and every day. Reflecting is very similar to riding a bike. After you learn what it looks like and how it is done, it comes very naturally. The earlier reflection is learned, the easier it will be to make it a habit. If you are going to cut something out of your day or your learning experience because of time, don't let it be reflection. Show your students how much you value their reflections by making it a priority. Just saying something is a priority isn't going to send a message. You have to show them it's a priority by doing it every single day.

Introduce Accountability Partners

Encourage your learners to have reflection accountability partners. When they need an opportunity to reflect on something that didn't go well or share something that did, they have someone who is always willing to listen. Doing so will help them work on communication skills and collaboration, and give them a very authentic reflection experience. For younger learners, you might give them talking points or conversation starters. Having an accountability partner will encourage them to make reflection a priority even when they are not being asked to reflect, encouraging ownership and self-awareness.

If you are going to cut something out of your day or your learning experience because of time, don't let it be reflection.

At first, students might not understand the purpose behind the accountability partners and might see this as silly or something that they can put on the back burner. It's important for educators to weave in opportunities for accountability partners to collaborate early on so that it becomes a habit and something that becomes valuable to them as learners. Through this experience, new friendships will be created, and reflection will be seen as a priority in the classroom.

Share Student Reflections

My students often reflected by writing blog posts. Student blogging is such a great way to encourage students to share their learning and gives them an authentic audience. In doing so, they are able to not only share their reflections, but also practice their writing skills and understand what it is like to write something that will be shared with an audience. Sometimes I would give my students a specific prompt or question. Other times, I just gave them an opportunity to share their learning however they thought was most appropriate. They loved reading each other's blog posts, and it was fun to hear them realize that they all connected differently with the learning. It was also fun to watch students who never worried about anything when turning in work all of a sudden become concerned about punctuation, vocabulary, and misspelled words. They understood that their work was going to be shared, and this gave them a reason to want to write well.

REFLECT

How comfortable are you when it comes to sharing your students' work? What can you do to move outside that comfort zone in a way that is best for you and your learners?

A NOTE ABOUT SHARING STUDENT WORK ONLINE

Sharing student work can be messy. There will be times when a parent is concerned, other teachers are concerned, and maybe even administration has questions about why student work is being shared for the world to see. The answer is simple. As addressed in my core beliefs, our learners deserve an authentic audience. They are familiar with creating for an audience. When they go home and post on social media, they are doing so in the hopes that they will have a very large audience. Social media isn't going anywhere. It's here to stay, and it's very important that learners realize that they can promote themselves positively by sharing their ideas, learning, and designs with others.

There's no doubt that it's important to teach students to be safe while sharing work publicly. It's important to have guidelines in place to encourage students to practice safely while they are online. For example, my students were never permitted to share their last names or their school's name. Digital citizenship was a priority in my classroom and something that I tried to weave into the things that we did on a daily basis. In doing so, my students understood what they were and were not allowed to do when sharing their work.

There are so many resources and tools that can be used to address digital citizenship. Although it's important to weave digital citizenship into the daily classroom experiences, there is also curriculum that has been created to help address specific areas of concern with today's learners. There are three specific resources that I think are best for addressing digital citizenship in the classroom:

- Common Sense Media (https://www.commonsensemedia.org): This resource includes an entire curriculum for K–12 learners, as well as parent resources, interactives for students, and so much more.
- Be Internet Awesome (https://beinternetawesome.withgoogle.com): Google's digital citizenship resource includes lesson plans most appropriate for grades 3–5 and is interactive.

- GoBubble (https://www.bubble.school): GoBubble is a great resource when encouraging students 13 years old and younger to share their work and ideas.

Other Valuable Reflection Tools

Another great way for students to reflect is to use Flipgrid (https://flipgrid.com). If you haven't heard of Flipgrid, you can thank me later. This is a wonderful tool that encourages and supports engagement and student reflection. As the educator, you create grids with topics. Within the topics, students can share ideas, thoughts, reflections, and learning that they have experienced. They simply click the green button, start recording, and share their insights. I love Flipgrid because it allows for instant feedback. As the teacher, you can watch their video and respond immediately within the platform to what was shared. The students can also leave feedback for each other, giving opportunities for collaboration and communication.

Remember to model reflection for your learners. If you encourage them to have reflection accountability partners, you should have one as well. Voxer is a great app that serves as a walkie-talkie on your smartphone. I have two reflection accountability partners who I vox after every speaking engagement, workshop, keynote, or writing session that I do. We talk about what went well, what didn't go well, and what I could have done differently to create an even better experience. I also continue to blog in order to reflect on things that are important to me and share my thoughts and reflections on social media like Facebook and Twitter. Utilizing these strategies gives me an outlet, places to record my thoughts, and something to look back at when I need ideas or inspiration. Reflection helps me see a situation for what it was after it has had time to marinate.

Reflection is a powerful tool when used the right way. Peter Pappas (2010) created a Reflection Taxonomy, which I believe helps educators and learners become more intentional when reflecting.

The taxonomy addresses student, teacher, and administration reflection and is structured to parallel Bloom's taxonomy. It's a great way to help students and educators understand the "what" and the "how" behind reflecting.

ENGAGE

 Visit https://peterpappas.com/2010/01/reflective-teacher-taxonomy-reflection.html. Reflect on something that you did today or recently in your own classroom. Go through the levels of reflection, answering them in a journal, on a blog, or with a reflection accountability partner.

I'm not sure that there is anything that we can do in the classroom more powerful than reflecting. Once learners begin to value reflection, we have set them up to value learning. And when they value learning, they will become lifelong learners willing to take risks knowing that it was more about the process all along.

REFLECT

Are you making reflection a priority in your classroom? If not, how can you help your learners focus on reflection instead of remembering?

_____

_____

_____

_____

Meaningful Technology

THERE is a lot of talk about technology in education right now. But just like everything that we do in the classroom, if the technology that we use isn't meaningful for our learners, it's a waste of our time and theirs. There are a lot of really cool tools out there for teachers to use. And there's no doubt that, just like everything else that we've discussed throughout this book, finding meaningful technology can be messy. It can be confusing, difficult, and even frustrating if you aren't exactly sure what you want technology to do for your learners.

REFLECT

What do you want technology to do for your learners? Have you made a meaningful technology checklist, or if you did, what would it look like?

_____

_____

_____

_____

_____

_____

There are three things that I always look for when it comes to finding and using educational technology tools. It's important that the technology that we choose:

1. engages and empowers our learners,
2. deepens their understanding, and
3. helps them make connections.

If technology does those things, there is every reason to use it. Although a tool doesn't have to do all of these things, it should do at least one to be considered meaningful.

Too often, we are using technology because we think our learners will be more engaged simply because they have a device in their hands. That is not the case. I have seen many engaging and empowering learning experiences that have not involved one piece of technology. I've also seen educators use many different tools and still not have learners who are engaged, much less empowered. Technology does not have to present for learning to take place, and learning will not always take place because technology is being used.

Technology Should Engage and Empower Learners

Just like any learning that happens in the classroom, technology should engage and empower today's learners. It should not simply replace a worksheet, but instead should create a completely new experience that can only be done because of the technology. Engaging technology is technology that involves learners or gives them a reason to want to be involved. It pulls them in and makes them see the learning from a different perspective. Technology that empowers not only involves learners, but also gives them an experience that they can apply outside of the classroom. Experiences that empower our learners provide the drive and connections that they need to apply what they have learned.

An example of meaningful technology that engages and empowers is connecting with experts outside of the classroom via technology. As discussed earlier in this book, connecting with experts can be a huge opportunity for learners to understand the "why" behind what is being learned. If an outside expert is able to create an experience that involves the learners and share how they use whatever it is that is being learned, students will be both engaged and empowered through the experience.

> Experiences that empower our learners provide the drive and connections that they need to apply what they have learned.

Backchannels also engage and empower learners as they multitask to share their thoughts and ideas while learning. Google Slides has a backchannel feature called Google Q&A, or you can even use a Twitter hashtag as a backchannel. It's simply a place for students to place their thoughts and reflections while an experience is happening. Just a reminder: It's never a good idea to leave a backchannel completely unmonitored. However, if done well, a backchannel can be a perfect place for students to make predictions, ask questions, and learn from others.

REFLECT

What is a tool that you are currently using or can use in your classroom that you believe engages and empowers your learners?

_____

_____

Technology Should Deepen Student Understanding

Meaningful technology also deepens understanding. Because of the tool being used, learners are able to truly understand what is being learned instead of simply recalling or regurgitating the information. Meaningful technology will also help learners who are ready to move beyond surface level and into those deeper levels where they can explore and dive into what is being learned.

Students can deepen their understanding by reflecting or thinking critically about what has been learned. Mensa for Kids (https://www.mensaforkids.org) is a wonderful website that helps students think critically about their learning by using TED Talks that are appropriate for students. Through this website, students choose a TED Talk to watch and are then given access to critical thinking questions and experiences that will help them take what they have learned to a deeper level.

TED-Ed (https://ed.ted.com) is another great way for students to deepen their understanding. TED-Ed offers videos for educators to use to engage their learners. After watching the video, learners are asked to think about what they've watched, discuss what was learned, and are given the opportunity to dig deeper to learn even more. Educators can customize the lessons or use them as they are. This tool is a perfect way to engage students and then give them opportunities to dive into what has been learned. Educators are also able to create their own lessons from scratch using TED-Ed.

REFLECT

What is a tool that you are currently using or can use in your classroom that you believe deepens the understanding of your learners?

_____

_____

Technology Should Help Learners Make Connections

Technology gives us a huge opportunity to help our learners make connections. One way to do this is to help students make connections with things that are meaningful and relevant to them. Video games are one thing that many learners like to do outside of school. Connecting what is being learned to designing a video game or asking students to create a video game to share their learning is one way to do this. Using tools like Scratch and Code.org, learners connect what is being learned through something that involves creativity, collaboration, and critical thinking. In doing so, the learning is solidified and an experience is created that will result in applying and understanding what was learned.

Virtual reality is another way for learners to make connections. As we discussed earlier, virtual reality has the potential to change education. Using tools like 360Cities, you can take students virtually anywhere in the world. You simply search for your location of choice and you will be provided with 360° images for your learners to experience. One of my favorite apps to share with educators is Figment AR. If you haven't seen it, prepare to be amazed. The app can be downloaded from the Apple App Store or the Google Play Store. Using this app, portals can be created in any location. This means that, when students use a device, your classroom will appear to have portals around the room that students can enter. You can then drop 360° images of any location into the portals, so that when students go through the portal, they feel as though they are actually there. For example, when you are explaining rural and urban areas to today's learners, they might not truly under-

> Help students make connections with things that are meaningful and relevant to them.

stand the difference between the two. Depending on where they live, they possibly have only experienced that area. But what if you used Figment AR to create portals that they could enter to experience and identify both rural and urban locations? As they enter the portals, students will be able to look around and will even be able to see back into the classroom when they hover over the portal again.

Imagine telling your students when they walk into class that there are portals that they will be able to see when they pick up their iPads. Just in doing this, you have their attention, and they can't wait to see what the rest of the class period has in store for them. They are either thinking that you have completely lost it and they are here to witness it, or there are really portals in the classroom and they are going to get to check them out. You can then ask them to go through the portals, look around, and find real examples of geome-try vocabulary. This will allow them to connect the learning and the words with an experience that they will remember forever. This connection is what will make the learning stick so that it is not just in their short-term memory but also their long-term memory.

REFLECT

What is a tool that you are currently using or can use in your classroom that you believe helps your learners make connections?

_____

_____

Be Purposeful in Finding Meaningful Technology

The key to finding meaningful technology for your classroom is being purposeful. Know what you want the tool to do. Do not use something simply because it's what everyone is talking about or because it's flashy. Be intentional when you are designing your learning experiences, and if the technology isn't going to impact the learning in a meaningful way, don't use it. Unfortunately, we've fallen into believing that simply using technology in the classroom will engage our learners. In fact, many of our learners prefer to not use technology in certain situations. Many of them prefer to read real books, not from a tablet. Some of them prefer to write rather than type on a keyboard. Although students need to practice technology skills, we shouldn't simply use technology tools for the sake of using them.

REFLECT

Can you think of a time that you used a popular technology tool and it didn't do what you had hoped? Do you think having a checklist will help?

_____

_____

_____

_____

Technology can take the learning to the next level. Use it because it will engage and empower students, deepen their understanding, and/or help them make connections (see Figure 7). Ask your students questions after using specific tools to gain feedback and insight into what impact it had on them as learners. And, if something that you used didn't work or didn't do any of the things that we talked about previously, don't use it again because the reality is that it would be a waste of time.

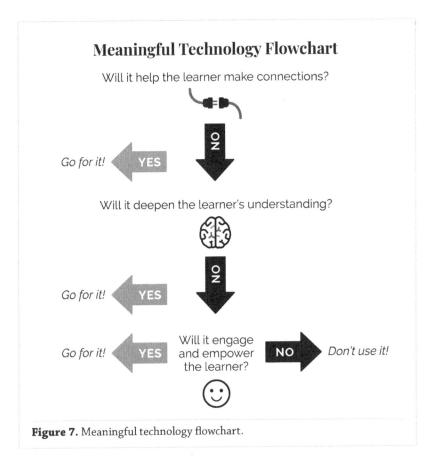

Figure 7. Meaningful technology flowchart.

Making Your Classroom a Meaningful Mess

MY hope is that as you've read through this book, you've realized that teaching needs to look very different. I hope that you have seen the strengths that this generation has and realized the impact that these students have the potential to make on our world if we simply give them the opportunity. The reality is that success in school doesn't match success outside of school. How can we make risk-taking, failure, reflection, grit, and passion priorities in the classroom so that today's learners are ready for their futures?

It will not happen in a classroom where the teacher is seen as the expert and the students are simply there to watch to the show. Messy, meaningful learning will only happen when we, as educators, let go of the wheel and allow our learners to drive. It's okay if you find yourself checking your seatbelt often and maybe even holding on for dear life in the beginning. But regardless of the fear and discomfort that we feel, we must know our students well, be willing to take risks, fail during the process, and design experiences that will engage and empower students through meaningful learning every single day.

Reignite Your Passion for Teaching

Throughout the book, we've talked about ways to help your learners find their passions and ignite their love of learning. But it's important for us to do the same as educators. It happens to almost every teacher. As I wrote in a recent blog post (McNair, 2017a):

> There comes a place in our career that the passion just isn't there. We forget why we do what we do. We become frustrated by expectations, paperwork, and standardized testing. We begin to fear that our voices cannot be heard and we begin to do day after day what we know isn't working and isn't best for our students. (para. 1)

Yet, as teachers, we know what students need (McNair, 2017). Passion drives us to want the best for our learners and encourages us to return to the classroom each day—even when we feel defeated. This passion might be a passion for impacting the future, a passion for inspiring the lives of your students, or a passion for engaging and empowering today's learners. Whatever that passion is, it exists and plays a role in how and

Passion drives us to want the best for our learners and encourages us to return to the classroom each day— even when we feel defeated.

what we do in our classrooms every day. Although passion exists in all teachers, I also believe that it can become stifled. The flame can flicker, and we begin to worry that it might actually be extinguished if we can't find a way to reignite the flame soon. But that flame can be reignited—even set ablaze—if you actively pursue the passion that you once had.

How do you find your way back to being the teacher you want to be instead of the teacher that you are expected to be? How do you become the teacher that your students need? In thinking about how I found my passion again, I realized that there were three things that helped me find my way. To find your passion, you must (McNair, 2017a):

1. take risks,
2. find your tribe, and
3. share your story.

REFLECT

How strong is your flame right now? Would you say it's brightly burning or barely blinking? How do you know?

_____

_____

_____

_____

Take Risks

Taking risks is not easy. Seth Godin said, "If it scares you, it might be a good thing to try." How often do you do things in your classroom that scare you? Remember, if you are consistently comfortable teaching this generation of learners, it might be time to take a risk (McNair, 2017a). Because society is changing so quickly and these learners are so different than past generations, you should be at least a little uncomfortable. With discomfort comes the need to move, to change. Allow your discomfort to push you outside of that comfort zone, and take the risks that you know are worth taking for you and your students. Be willing to learn with your students, and do whatever it takes to make the learning meaningful and relevant every single day.

EMPOWER

What was the last thing that you did in your classroom that scared you? What can you do fairly soon that scares you a little?

_____

_____

_____

_____

_____

_____

_____

Find Your Tribe

Being a connected educator changes everything (McNair, 2017a). Finding your people, knowing them well, and trusting them enough to share and grow together is a game changer. Likeminded people give you the boost and support that you need to go beyond what's comfortable and take the risks that will stretch you as an educator. In connecting, you begin to see what education can be, instead of what it is in your classroom, on your campus, or in your district. Oftentimes, when you begin to do things differently, you might feel alone. When you feel like an island, it's time to build a bridge. Build a bridge that connects you to other educators who inspire and encourage you.

Finding your tribe gives you a support system that encourages you, pushes you, and supports you to do the hard things. And when you begin to do the hard things, like allowing students to drive the learning, seeing yourself as a facilitator, and allowing them to learn by doing, you begin to realize that challenges are opportunities to learn and grow as you move toward finding your passion for teaching again.

ENGAGE

If you are not on Twitter, create an account now that you use only to connect with other educators all over the world. Follow me on Twitter, @mcnairan3, and I will be happy to follow you back and show you the ropes!

Share Your Story

Education is difficult. Teaching is mentally and sometimes physically exhausting (McNair, 2017a). Bringing your A game every day is not easy, and developing original ideas on a consistent basis is even harder. You don't have to. Be transparent and ask for help. So many educators are sharing their stories. It might be on Twitter, on a blog, or at a conference. It doesn't matter how, but find ways to share what you are doing in your classroom. Share what works . . . share what doesn't work. Just share. In doing so, you will begin to see that reflection is imperative for you as an educator and gives you an opportunity to see your teaching from a different perspective. And let's face it, if you don't share your story, someone else will.

> Likeminded people give you the boost and support that you need to go beyond what's comfortable and take the risks that will stretch you as an educator.

As educators, there's a lot that we can complain about in today's classrooms. But the reality is that there has never been a more exciting time to be a teacher. Let's step back from the negativity and do whatever it takes to provide our students with meaningful learning experiences. Our students deserve passionate teachers who believe in them and all that they bring to the table. Passionate educators create passionate learners who have the potential to change the world.

Embrace Change

The school game that we are playing right now does not simulate the real world. Because of this, we should never assume that we know a student's potential based on how well he or she plays school. Some of the students who do not play the school game well are the very ones who are finding the most success outside of school. You see, in order to be successful in today's world, one must be willing to take risks and try new things. If we continue to make school a place where learners are expected to be compliant and failure is seen as a negative experience, we have to be willing to accept that we are simply preparing them for a test—and not the real world.

As educators, we have the privilege of teaching every single learner who walks through our classroom doors. If our students know every single thing that we have already planned to teach, then we have to design experiences that will enable them to go deeper. If they are behind where we are and it seems like there is no way that they will ever catch up, we have to design experiences that will help them make the connections that they need to make to see progress. We are accountable to a lot of people. We are accountable to our state, our administration, and even to parents. But our ultimately accountability is to the learners who come to our classrooms each and every day. And they deserve educators who are willing to take risks in order to create a meaningful mess that will result in meaningful learning.

Speaking from experience, it's easy to become frazzled, stressed, and worn out from teaching a classroom of 20–30 different learners for 5 days a week. I really believe that oftentimes we feel frazzled and stressed because we are pushing against what today's learners need rather than leaning into it. Brené Brown said, "Lean into the discomfort of the work." By leaning into what today's learners bring to the table rather than pushing against it, we will find our jobs much more fulfilling and satisfying, rather than exhausting and unpleasant.

> It's important that we teach in such a way that each student thinks that he or she is our favorite.

It is heartbreaking to hear students say things like, "My teacher doesn't like me," or "I don't want to go to school." School should and could be a place where every learner wants to be. It's important that we teach in such a way that each student thinks that he or she is our favorite. Think about it. Students think they are the favorite when their teachers know them well, treat them with respect, and value their opinion. Shouldn't every learner have that experience in the classroom?

Change in education will not come from us sitting around talking about it or even simply reading books about it. Real change will begin to happen when educators, like yourself, begin to do what it takes to reach a generation of learners who deserve an entirely different learning experience than any of us were given. Change will come when we recognize that our current practices simply will not work and we become willing to shift our mindsets from what we've always done to what works. Finally, change will come when we are willing to step outside of our comfort zones and into a meaningful mess that will take learning to the next level.

Final Thoughts

I've asked lots of questions throughout this book. I've asked you to reflect, engage, and be empowered. I have one final question to ask you as we end our time together and you prepare to take what you've read and use it to transform your classroom. My final question is this . . .

How will you use messy learning experiences to give today's learners what they deserve?

Be you and give your learners opportunities to be themselves. Today's learners need passionate educators who are willing to be who they are. You are enough and your passion for what you do is enough to change everything. So, take some time to sit down and remember why you began teaching. What is it about teaching that you absolutely love, and how can you use that to create real change in your own classroom? Be okay with your meaningful mess, knowing that is more about being real than being right. In doing so, you will begin to create a culture in your classroom that is best for you and your students.

> You are enough and your passion for what you do is enough is to change everything.

Invest in your learners. Pour into them in such a way that every single one of them feels as though he or she is the favorite student.

In return, they will find reasons to invest in the learning that is happening in the classroom every day. We can all be a mess sometimes. Those messes often have nothing to do with school but impact what happens in the classroom every day. Use your mess to create meaning and give your students opportunities to do the same.

It's your call. The ball is your court. You can continue to do what's comfortable, or you can do what's right. Be brave, take risks, and let's make education all that it should be for today's learners. Chase after your purpose with a fearless willingness to do what it takes to create real change. They deserve it—and so do you.

References

Adams, S. (2014). The 10 skills employers most want in 2015 graduates. *Forbes*. Retrieved from https://www.forbes.com/sites/susanadams/2014/11/12/the-10-skills-employers-most-want-in-2015-graduates

BCM Partnership. (2015). *How to communicate with Gen Z* [Video file]. Retrieved from https://www.youtube.com/watch?v=LmNzZf0996o

Beall, G. (2017). 8 key differences between gen z and millennials. *HuffPost*. Retrieved from https://www.huffingtonpost.com/george-beall/8-key-differences-between_b_12814200.html

Brejcha, L. (2018). *Makerspaces in school: A month-by-month schoolwide model for building meaningful makerspaces.* Waco, TX: Prufrock Press.

Buchanan, A. (2016). Redefining success in education: The benefit mindset. *Medium*. Retrieved from https://medium.com/benefit-mindset/redefining-success-in-education-the-benefit-mindset-6dc5743733f6

Burgess, D. (2012). *Teach like a pirate: Increase student engagement, boost your creativity, and transform your life as an educator.* San Diego, CA: Burgess Consulting.

Connell, G. (2014). Geography skills soar with mystery Skype. *Scholastic.* Retrieved from https://www.scholastic.com/teachers/blog-posts/genia-connell/geography-skills-soar-mystery-skype

Donally, J. (2018). *Learning transported: Augmented, virtual and mixed reality for all classrooms.* Portland, OR: International Society for Technology in Education.

Edutopia. (2015). *Having students lead parent conferences.* Retrieved from https://www.edutopia.org/practice/student-led-conferences-empowerment-and-ownership

The Foundation for Critical Thinking. (n.d.). *Defining critical thinking.* Retrieved from http://www.criticalthinking.org/pages/defining-critical-thinking/766

Fryer, J. (2017). This 12-year-old is creating an app for disabled people. *NBC News.* Retrieved from https://www.nbcnews.com/feature/inspiring-america/12-year-old-creating-app-disabled-people-n766326

Goldin, K. (2017). From gap to gen z: Why collaboration is more important than ever. *Forbes.* Retrieved from https://www.forbes.com/sites/karagoldin/2017/11/10/from-gap-to-gen-z-why-collaboration-is-more-important-than-ever/#239fc2944af8

Hodgson, L. (2012). *Gen Z wants to make a difference, not a profit* [Web log post]. Retrieved from https://www.huffingtonpost.com/louise-hodgson/make-differences-not-profits_b_1919251.html

Kozinsky, S. (2017). How Generation Z is shaping the change in education. *Forbes.* Retrieved from https://www.forbes.com/sites/sievakozinsky/2017/07/24/how-generation-z-is-shaping-the-change-in-education

McKale, L. (2016). *Leaders vs. managers: 17 traits that set them apart [infographic].* Retrieved from https://www.resourcefulmanager.com/leaders-vs-managers

McNair, A. (2015). A mystery Skype to remember [Web log post]. Retrieved from http://ameaningfulmess.blogspot.com/2015/11/teachers-learning-from-students.html

McNair, A. (2017a). *3 ways to find your passion for teaching (again)* [Web log post]. Retrieved from http://ameaningfulmess.blogspot.com/2017/09/3-ways-to-find-your-passion-for.html

McNair, A. (2017b). *Genius hour: Passion projects that ignite innovation and student inquiry.* Waco, TX: Prufrock Press.

McNair, A. (2018). *What are your core beliefs?* [Web log post]. Retrieved from http://ameaningfulmess.blogspot.com/2018/08/what-are-your-core-beliefs.html

National Education Association. (2010). *Preparing 21st century students for a global society: An educator's guide to the "four Cs".* Retrieved from http://www.nea.org/assets/docs/A-Guide-to-Four-Cs.pdf

National Ocean and Atmospheric Administration. (2018). *How much of the ocean have we explored?* Retrieved from https://oceanservice.noaa.gov/facts/exploration.html

Newnham, D. (2016). From Summly to Silicon Valley: The teen who sold his app for $30 million. *Medium.* Retrieved from https://medium.com/the-mission/from-summly-to-silicon-valley-interview-with-nick-daloisio-who-sold-his-app-business-for-30-686a32ac1af8

Pappas, P. (2010). *A taxonomy of reflection: critical thinking for students, teachers, and principals (part 1).* Retrieved from http://peterpappas.com/2010/01/taxonomy-reflection-critical-thinking-students-teachers-principals.html

Patel, D. (2017). 5 differences between marketing to millennials vs. gen z. *Forbes.* Retrieved from https://www.forbes.com/sites/deeppatel/2017/11/27/5-d%E2%80%8Bifferences-%E2%80%8Bbetween-%E2%80%8Bmarketing-%E2%80%8Bto%E2%80%8B-m z%E2%80%8Billennials-v%E2%80%8Bs%E2%80%8B-%E2%80%8Bgen-z/#ac442d72c9ff

Premack, R. (2018). Millennials love their brands, Gen Zs are terrified of college debt, and 6 other ways Gen Zs and millennials are totally

different. *Business Insider*. Retrieved from https://www.business insider.com/gen-zs-habits-different-from-millennials-2018-6

Rampton, J. (2016). Businesses that took huge risks that paid off. *Inc*. Retrieved from https://www.inc.com/john-rampton/15-business es-that-took-huge-risks-that-paid-off.html

Rendina, D. (2015). *Defining makerspaces: What the research says* [Web log post]. Retrieved from http://renovatedlearning.com/ 2015/04/02/defining-makerspaces-part-1

Sneckner, S. (2015). *How does Apple conduct its employees' performance appraisals?* Retrieved from https://www.quora.com/How-does-Apple-conduct-its-employees-performance-appraisals

United Nations. (2015). *The global goals for sustainable development*. Retrieved from https://www.globalgoals.org

Appendix

Additional Resources

360Cities
https://www.360cities.net

Be Internet Awesome
https://beinternetawesome.
withgoogle.com/en

Book Creator
https://bookcreator.com

ChessKid
https://www.chesskid.com

Code.org
https://code.org

Common Sense Media
https://www.commonsense
media.org

Duolingo
https://www.duolingo.com

DogoNews
https://www.dogonews.com

Empatico
https://empatico.org

Flipgrid
https://flipgrid.com

Global Goals
https://www.globalgoals.org

GoBubble
https://www.bubble.school

Google Slides
https://www.google.com/slides/about

Kidblog
https://kidblog.org/home

Mensa for Kids
https://www.mensaforkids.org

Nearpod
https://nearpod.com

Newsela
https://newsela.com

Scratch
https://scratch.mit.edu

Skype for the Classroom
https://education.microsoft.com/skype-in-the-classroom/overview

StoryJumper
https://www.storyjumper.com

TED-Ed
https://ed.ted.com

The DIRT Survey
https://www.iidc.indiana.edu/cedir/dirt/index.php

Twitter
https://twitter.com

Voxer
https://www.voxer.com

Weebly for Education
https://education.weebly.com

Wonderopolis
https://www.wonderopolis.org

YouTube
https://www.youtube.com

Book Study Questions

These questions can be used for reflection, a traditional book study, or a digital book study through social media. If you would like access to images to use along with the questions for social media, visit http://www.andimcnair.com/a-meaningful-mess.html.

Chapter 1: What Makes a Mess Meaningful?

1. How do you feel about taking risks in the classroom?
2. Do you believe that today's learners deserve more? Why or why not?
3. What's the difference between messy learning and messy teaching?
4. Is your work meaningful to you? How do you know?
5. What do you remember about your school experience?

Chapter 2: Getting to Know Gen Z

1. How is Gen Z different from learners in the past?
2. What is Gen Z's biggest strength?
3. What is Gen Z's biggest weakness?
4. Does this generation of learners make you uncomfortable?
5. Which truth about Gen Z was most surprising, and why?

Chapter 3: Giving Students What They Deserve

1. How do you know when a learner is prepared to dive deeper?
2. What are your core beliefs?
3. Which suggestion from this chapter can you implement right away?
4. What opportunities can you give your learners to see failure for what it really is?

5. How can you make instant feedback a priority in your classroom?

Chapter 4: Letting Go of Control

1. How difficult is it for you to let go of control?
2. How many rules do you have, and how would you feel about only having one?
3. Would you want to be a learner in your own classroom? Why or why not?
4. Is your classroom student-driven or learner-driven?
5. How can you begin to let students D.R.I.V.E. their learning in your classroom?

Chapter 5: Empowerment Versus Compliance

1. Were you an empowered or compliant learner in school? How do you know?
2. Do you see yourself as a manager of students or a leader of learners?
3. Do you give more grades or more feedback? What's the difference?
4. What can you do to prepare your learners for life outside of the classroom?
5. How comfortable are you allowing learners to lead their own learning?

Chapter 6: The 3 E's: Designing Meaningful Learning Experiences

1. Are your learners self-aware?
2. Which of the 3 E's will have the most impact in your classroom?

3. How can you engage your learners as soon as they enter the room?
4. What experiences can you create to cause learners to want to invest?
5. How can you empower your students to take their learning beyond the walls of the classroom?

Chapter 7: The 4 C's + 1 R: Collaboration, Communication, Creativity, Critical Thinking, and Reflection

1. Why are the 4 C's + 1 R important for today's learners?
2. What's the difference between collaboration and group work?
3. What is a practical way that you can allow your learners to practice communication in the classroom?
4. How often do you allow your students to produce rather than consume?
5. How can you encourage more critical thinking in your classroom?

Chapter 8: Learning by Doing: Genius Hour and Meaningful Makerspaces

1. How is learning by application different than learning by consumption?
2. How do you feel about giving your learners an opportunity to learn by pursuing their passions during the school day?
3. What role does purpose play in your classroom, and how can you make it a priority?
4. What's the difference between a Makerspace and a meaningful Makerspace?
5. How you can you focus on the process rather than the product and encourage your learners to do the same?

Chapter 9: Going Global

1. How can you use the Global Goals in your classroom to encourage your learners to create change?
2. How can you use virtual learning to help students make connections and experience learning?
3. Have you used outside experts before in your classroom? What was the impact?
4. What impact do you think outside experts can have in your classroom?
5. How do you feel about connecting your classroom globally and what impact might it have on your learners?

Chapter 10: Reflection Versus Remembering

1. Why should learners reflect rather than remember?
2. How can you, as an educator, model reflection?
3. Do you think accountability partners will work in your classroom? Why or why not
4. How do you feel about sharing student reflections?
5. What reflection tool do you feel will be most valuable in your classroom, and why?

Chapter 11: Meaningful Technology

1. What do you believe makes technology meaningful?
2. Are you using technology to engage and empower your learners? How do you know?
3. Why is it important for learners to deepen their understanding?
4. What is a technology tool that you have used in your classroom to help learners make connections?
5. How do you know if technology is not meaningful for your learners?

Chapter 12: Making Your Classroom a Meaningful Mess

1. How can you reignite your passion for teaching?
2. What risks can you take in your classroom to create real change and empower your learners?
3. What can you do today to find your tribe?
4. How can you share your story so that we can learn from you?
5. How do you feel about change?
6. Are you willing to chase after your purpose to do what it takes to create real change?

About the Author

Andi McNair is the Digital Innovation Specialist at ESC Region 12 in Waco, TX. Before working at the center, she taught elementary and gifted/talented students at a small rural school in Texas. Andi was in the classroom for a total of 16 years before pursuing her passion to change education by giving educators practical ways to create experiences that will engage and empower this generation of learners. Andi has spoken at many conferences and education service centers, and has worked with many school districts to provide innovative learning experiences for their students. She was named one of the Top People in Education to Watch in 2016 by the Academy of Education Arts and Sciences. Andi's first book, *Genius Hour: Passion Projects That Ignite Innovation and Student Inquiry*, is winner of the 2019 Teachers' Choice Award for Professional Development.

As an educator, Andi is passionate about using meaningful technology in the classroom and finding innovative ways to engage and empower today's learners. She believes that the students we are educating today are unique and we must be creative in designing experiences that will engage and empower them as learners.

To learn more about Andi or to invite her to speak on your campus, in your district, or at your event, please visit http://www. andimcnair.com.